MARKETING
MASTERS

MARKETING MASTERS

SECRETS OF AMERICA'S BEST COMPANIES

GENE WALDEN AND EDMUND O. LAWLER

HarperBusiness
A Division of HarperCollinsPublishers

First paperback edition published 1994.

Designed by Alma Hochhauser Orenstein

The Library of Congress has catalogued the hardcover edition as follows:

Walden, Gene.
  Marketing masters : secrets of America's best companies / Gene Walden, Edmund O. Lawler
    p. cm.
  ISBN 0-88730-590-3
  1. Marketing—United States. 2. Success in business—United States. I. Lawler, Edmund O. II. Title.
HF5415.1.W35 1993
658.8—dc20   92-54750

ISBN 0-88730-690-X (pbk.)

94 95 96 97 98 ❖/CW 10 9 8 7 6 5 4 3 2 1

To Priscilla, Griffin and Bryan
— EDMUND O. LAWLER

To the Gym Rats of Minnehaha
— GENE WALDEN

CONTENTS

keters at Walgreen, Oshkosh, Kinder-Care, Zeos, Aveda, Subway, and McDonald's have learned.

Marketing products as complex as telecommunications systems, computer hardware and software, and specialty chemicals takes more than a catchy jingle. Marketers at PictureTel, Software Publishing, Truevision, Sullivan Dental Products, Nalco Chemical, and Octel Communications describe the challenge of selling business to business.

Service marketers have been helping corporations do everything from paying their employees to running their computers. Trendsetters include Automatic Data Processing (ADP), Electronic Data Services (EDS), Devon Direct, Centex Telemanagement, and The Interface Group.

Down-and-all-but-out companies like retailer Sharper Image, deluxe shoemaker Allen-Edmonds, brewer Rolling Rock, computer retailer Connecting Point, and terminal manufacturer Link Technologies have all come back strong by revamping their marketing strategies. For nonprofit marketers, the El Paso YWCA is a sparkling example of how to do it right.

U.S. companies like Medtronic, Brock Control Systems, Houston-based Methodist Hospital, and Sybaritic have overcome a host of economic, political, and cultural obstacles to penetrate foreign markets successfully.

A final summary on how the best marketers make it happen.

Photographs follow pages 80

ACKNOWLEDGMENTS

WE WOULD LIKE TO THANK the many men and women who contributed their knowledge, experience, and insights to this book, including (listed in order of appearance in the book) the following:

Wolfgang R. Schmitt, president and CEO
Rubbermaid, Inc.
Don Tyson, chairman and CEO
Tyson Foods
David Ridley, marketing director
Southwest Airlines Company
Mel Masters, chairman, president, and CEO
LaserMaster Technology
Pierluigi Zappacosta, president and CEO
Logitech
Fabio Righi, vice president of marketing
Logitech
Kathleen E. Synnott, vice president of worldwide marketing
Mailing Systems Division
Pitney Bowes, Inc.
Daniel C. Ferguson, CEO
Newell Company
H. L. Tower, chairman
Stanhome, Inc.

Gene Freedman, president
Enesco Corporation
Dane Miller, president and CEO
Biomet
Steve Poole, director of public relations
Gerber Products Company
Vernon A. Brunner, executive vice president of marketing
Walgreen Company
Laurie Meyer, manager of corporate communications
Walgreen Company
Douglas W. Hyde, president and CEO
Oshkosh B'Gosh, Inc.
John Kaegi, senior vice president of marketing
Kinder-Care Learning Centers
Greg Herrick, chairman, president, and CEO ·
Zeos International
Horst Rechelbacher, founder, president, and CEO
Aveda Corporation
Fred DeLuca, president
Subway Sandwiches
David Green, senior vice president of marketing
McDonald's Corporation
Robert F. Mitro, vice president of sales and marketing
PictureTel Corporation
Fred M. Gibbons, president and CEO
Software Publishing Corporation
Cathleen Asch, CEO
Truevision
Dennis Collins, marketing director
Truevision
Robert J. Sullivan, chairman and CEO
Sullivan Dental
Robert E. Doering, president and COO
Sullivan Dental
W. Steven Weeber, group vice president
Nalco Chemical Company
John Berthoud, marketing director
Nalco Chemical Company
Ali D. Ata, manager of corporate marketing systems

Nalco Chemical Company
Douglas Chance, president and CEO
Octel Communications
Rob Reid, vice president of marketing
Octel Communications
Josh S. Weston, chairman and CEO
Automatic Data Processing, Inc.
Barry Sullivan, director of marketing
Electronic Data Services
Ron Greene, principal
Devon Direct
Jim Perry, principal
Devon Direct
Carol Krane, vice president of sales and marketing
Centex Telecommunications
Sheldon Adelson, chairman and CEO
The Interface Group
Richard Schwab, group vice president
The Interface Group
John Stollenwerk, president
Allen-Edmonds Shoes
Richard Thalheimer, chairman and president
Sharper Image Corporation
John Chappell, marketing director
Rolling Rock
Gary Held, former president
Connecting Point computer stores
Myrna Deckert, executive director
El Paso YWCA
Charles T. Comiso, president
Link Technologies
William W. George, president and CEO
Medtronic, Inc.
Richard Brock, chairman and CEO
Brock Control
Wayne Webb, manager of international development
Brock Control
Steve Daffer, president
Sybaritic, Inc.

José Nuñez, vice president of international affairs
Methodist Hospital
Houston, Texas
Patricia Chalupsky, manager of international patient services
Methodist Hospital
Houston, Texas

Also, special thanks to our manager, Peter Miller of the PMA
Agency.

INTRODUCTION:
DEFINING <u>BEST</u>

Any fool can paint a picture, but it takes a wise man to sell it.

—SAMUEL BUTLER (1835–1902)

IN THIS BOOK WE HAVE PROFILED more than three dozen companies from the well known, like Rubbermaid and McDonald's, to the obscure. If these are, indeed, America's "best" companies, what constitutes *best?* Is it size? Sales? Earnings growth, stability, stock growth, corporate ethics, efficiency, financial strength, management, or industry standing? *Best,* by its very nature, defies objectivity. *Best* is essentially what's best in the eyes of the beholder, but in *Marketing Masters,* Ed Lawler and I have followed some specific criteria while casting a wide net.

In my earlier book, *The 100 Best Stocks to Own in America* (rev. ed., 1991), I defined *best* as a combination of stock growth, earnings growth, dividend yield, and long-term consistency. Companies were carefully screened for financial performance over a full decade and ranked methodically from one to one hundred based on a preset scoring formula. *Best* had a clear purpose: What well-established, publicly traded companies had made the most money for investors? In *Marketing Masters,* we are trying to serve a broader purpose, although we *have* included some of the top companies from *The 100 Best Stocks.* Rubbermaid, McDonald's, Medtronic, Tyson Foods, Newell, Pitney Bowes, Stanhome, Automatic Data Processing, and Walgreen were all featured there. Many others from that list would have fit in nicely here as well. But we wanted to stretch our definition of *best* to include a diverse group of smaller companies, because that is where the real hope for American business lies—with the dynamic, emerging growth companies.

We selected companies in varying stages of their corporate development and from a full spectrum of industries. Obviously, we've included a fair representation of prominent blue chip companies that are widely recognized as leaders in their markets. But we have also included some younger emerging companies, both private and publicly traded firms, that are niche market leaders trying to hold on to that leadership role in the face of intense competition—or trying to diversify into other related areas. We've even included a few fallen market leaders who are battling their ways back to the top.

The objective of our selection process was to present a broad view of marketing for a wide range of readers—from the home-office entrepreneur to the small business marketing chief to the *Fortune* 500 CEO. In deciding on the mix of companies to feature, we made our selections based on a few key assumptions: that even the smallest business can benefit from the marketing lessons of the nation's most successful blue chip companies, that some of the smaller leading-edge companies often tend to be among the most creative marketers as well, that the lessons learned through failure and adversity can be just as important as the lessons of success, and that effective marketing is essential to all businesses of all sizes in all pursuits. As Robert Louis Stevenson once put it, "Everyone lives by selling something."

In short, what we looked for in choosing the companies for this book were businesses that have relied on quality, innovation, and marketing excellence to establish themselves as leaders in their respective industries. There are companies like Allen-Edmonds, the manufacturer of the world's best dress shoes; Tyson Foods, which sells more chickens than other company in the world; Southwest Airlines, which has posted more consecutive years of profitability than any other American airline; PictureTel, which is the leading manufacturer of picture phones; The Interface Group, the nation's leading trade show organizer; Medtronic, the world's dominant heart pacemaker manufacturer; and more than thirty other great companies with compelling stories to share of their challenges and achievements in the business of marketing.

MARKETING
MASTERS

CULTIVATING THE
MARKETING MIND-SET

MARKETING THEORY ABOUNDS with a multitude of fundamental concepts: cost-based analysis, competitive depositioning, psychological repositioning, product differentiation, and demographic intrapersonal evaluation.

But real marketing, in the flesh, has little to do with the rules and precepts of marketing theory. In the day-to-day business of peddling goods and services, the great companies—those that manage to sustain their growth through good times and bad—are constantly rewriting the rule book, not following it.

"The whole issue of keeping ahead of change, understanding it, dealing with it and adapting to it is a key to survival in our business," says Oshkosh B'Gosh president and CEO Douglas Hyde. "You must be willing to embrace change and deal with it. I am constantly having to remind myself that this is a new year. Don't assume that because something worked five years ago it will work again today—because it probably won't."

"We don't operate from a five-year marketing plan," agrees Biomet CEO Dane Miller. "We're constantly looking for new areas of growth." Indeed, marketing of the 1990s is more than advertising and more than selling. In studying the success of dozens of the most profitable companies in America—from emerging growth companies to multibillion dollar blue chips—we found that they shared one common characteristic: adaptability. The great companies see change as an ally, a force not to be feared but to be welcomed and exploited.

"We operate on the premise that our job is to identify trends," says Rubbermaid president and CEO Wolfgang Schmitt. "We've come to the conclusion, after many years, that we've never met a trend we didn't like."

Trends can be fickle, however. They can change in a heartbeat, but the great companies rarely miss a cue. "We manage from a daily, weekly, monthly, yearly basis as to what trends are happening on each individual product we carry," says Walgreen marketing chief Vernon A. Brunner.

Sometimes marketing adaptability can mean totally revamping the nature and dynamics of the entire company.

For eighty years Oshkosh was strictly in the business of selling clothing for farmers—until the company stumbled on a need for sturdy children's apparel. Now children's clothing constitutes 96 percent of the company's business.

Zeos International initially entered the computer business as a subcontractor, building circuit boards for other manufacturers. But after a sluggish start, founder Greg Herrick tried to shore up revenues by running a couple of magazine ads touting a line of Zeos personal computers. The calls poured in in such great volume that Herrick's ear literally began bleeding from holding the phone. Personally painful discovery that it was, it opened Herrick's eyes to the company's true strength. Now Zeos sells personal computers by the thousands per week.

Often great marketing means going against all conventional wisdom—contracting when everyone else says expand, expanding when everyone else is pulling back. At Enesco Corporation, a subsidiary of giftware manufacturer Stanhome, Inc., founder Gene Freedman recalls the phenomenal success of his Precious Moments line of porcelain figurines. Shortly after the introduction of the collection, sales soared and stores began raising their orders. The company suddenly found itself in short supply. Freedman's staff urged him to step up production to meet the demand. He cut back instead. He put tighter reins on the distribution, cut out the wholesalers, and set strict limits for retailers. "I must admit," says Freedman, "I had a lot of differences with my staff." But his decision proved a stroke of genius, as Precious Moments soon became the number one collectibles line in the world, grossing more than $100 million a year.

Freedman is not the only executive to turn his back on conventional wisdom in shaping marketing policy. When Sharper Image founder Richard Thalheimer decided to feature a gel insole for shoes in one of his recent catalogs, he recalls that "nobody in the company thought it would sell. They all laughed at it." But Thalheimer got the last laugh. Within the first year, the insoles were moving at a rate of thirty thousand pairs per month—the company's top seller. "It was funny," says Thalheimer, "when I'd ask the buyers in my company about a trade show, if they said, 'Oh no, there's nothing there,' that was a clue to me that I should probably go. . . . I found that it was at the smaller shows that no one else cared about where I could find the most terrific products."

Aveda founder Horst Rechelbacher recalls that when he first tried to peddle his all-natural hair care products in the 1970s, "people looked at me like I was crazy. The salespeople didn't want to hear what I had to say." Now the products are sold in some twenty-five thousand salons nationwide.

When Subway founder Fred DeLuca announced his long-term goal in 1982 of expanding from two hundred restaurants to five thousand restaurants by 1994, he remembers that "everyone looked at me like I was nuts." But Subway was up to seven thousand outlets by the end of 1992—well ahead of his initial goal.

While high-tech heavyweights like IBM and Digital Electronics were slugging it out in the main-frame manufacturing business, Ross Perot was quietly cutting his own slice of the computer revolution—customer service. Electronic Data Systems, the company Perot founded in 1962, doesn't build computers, but it takes in more than $7 billion a year in revenue providing a variety of computer services for its client companies.

In this age of focus groups, regional rollouts, and rigorous consumer test marketing, Rubbermaid introduces hundreds of new products a year without soliciting the input of a single consumer. Instead, everything is tested in-house to keep the competition at bay and hasten product introductions. The company can move a product from concept to store shelf in as little as twenty weeks—and still hits pay dirt with nine out of ten of its new introductions.

At the other end of the spectrum, Tyson Foods may test as many as one thousand variations of chicken patties (some in-house, some in focus groups, some in regional rollouts) before selecting a single one for introduction on a national basis.

The purpose of this book is to open your mind to new angles, new avenues, and new approaches to long-standing marketing challenges. In the pages that follow, we profile more than three dozen fast-growing companies from virtually every industrial segment—computer and software makers; medical products firms; retailers; food, clothing, consumer, and business product manufacturers; restaurants; hospitals; airlines; and service companies—to offer the broadest possible perspective on marketing in the 1990s. We reveal the stories, the strategies, and even the very thought processes behind these successful marketing campaigns.

Although you may well glean from their insights a fair share of marketing ideas that you can apply immediately to your own business, the long-term benefits should be far greater. The cumulative effect of studying the secrets of these great companies should be a new marketing mind-set; a new approach; a new way of attacking each problem, each opportunity, and each new marketplace challenge that comes your way.

LAUNCHING AGAINST ALL ODDS

OF THE MORE THAN THIRTEEN THOUSAND new products rolled out each year, only a few sell well enough to pay back the cost of bringing them to market. A new product launch—from research and development to national advertising and sales support—can run into the millions of dollars. To a great degree, the profitability of most manufacturers depends on the success rate of their new products. No company hits pay dirt with every new launch, but the best manage to keep the percentage of winners at a profitable level.

"New products are like a baseball player," says Tyson Foods founder Don Tyson. "You may not hit a home run every time, but you had better have a pretty good batting average or the stores are not going to invite you back." Tyson does chicken several hundred ways for its various retail, restaurant, and institutional customers. "Once we have a winner," adds Tyson president Leland Tollett, "we ask ourselves what else can we do with it. By putting money into products that are basically offshoots of what we've already done, we're able to diversify with minimal risk." Brand extension is a key strategy for many other top companies as well. Logitech, the computer mouse manufacturer, makes a mouse to meet nearly every taste—including the Kidz Mouse, a cordless mouse, and a mouse designed strictly for southpaws.

Rubbermaid maintains its edge by beating the competition to market. LaserMaster Technology, the high-speed laser printer manufacturer, anticipates printing problems created by the quick turnover in computer software applications and aims to be the first to market with equipment that solves those problems.

Airline travel has its own launch dynamics. Southwest Airlines, the only airline that's been profitable every year for the past two decades, has achieved an outstanding success rate in establishing new routes by offering fares low enough to encourage travelers to go by plane instead of by car.

Rubbermaid president and CEO Wolfgang Schmitt calls new products "the lifeblood of our business"—as they are with many manufacturers. It's a company's ability to bring those new products to market successfully that separates the great companies from the rest.

> We introduce every new product on a full rollout, national basis. We put ourselves under a lot of pressure by not test marketing. But it makes us do a better job up front of carefully validating that the product meets the needs of the consumer.
>
> —WOLFGANG R. SCHMITT,
> PRESIDENT AND CEO OF RUBBERMAID, INC.

When your company's products are synonymous with virtues like durability and quality, more than a few competitors are eager to piggyback on your handiwork. Rubbermaid stays ahead of its copycat competitors by being first to the retailer's shelves with a blizzard of trend-conscious new products for the home, yard, playroom, and workplace.

Nobody rolls out new products like Rubbermaid, which in 1992 introduced about 360 new products—nearly one for every day of the year. The Wooster, Ohio–based maker of utilitarian rubber and plastics goods packs its new product pipeline to meet its ambitious goal of generating 30 percent of its annual sales from products introduced over the previous five years. Rubbermaid's success with new products has enabled it to set new sales records for forty years straight.

Speed is one of the key ingredients to Rubbermaid's new product marketing success, explains Wolfgang R. Schmitt, who in 1991 was named president and CEO of the $1.7 billion company. "Today, the time between the flash of a new idea and actually getting a new product on the store shelves can be as little as twenty weeks," says Schmitt. "The average range is thirty to fifty weeks. An entire product line takes about two to three years to establish. We've been consistently reducing that time to market." Being quick to market not only reinforces Rubbermaid's reputation for innovation but also allows the company to grab the higher profit margins inherent in the early stages of a product's life cycle.

Rubbermaid gets to market ahead of the crowd for three key reasons:

- New products are the responsibility of a special business team, a sort of SWAT team from a variety of disciplines within the company, that nurtures a product from the point of trend identification to product introduction. The entrepreneurially minded teams are given enormous leeway and are not subject to "superfluous" examination by Rubbermaid executives, according to Schmitt.

- Rubbermaid eschews the conventional tack of test marketing a new product in a city or cities whose demographics are characteristic of the nation as a whole. The company doesn't want to show its hand to the other players who could then launch a preemptive strike.

- The company has invested heavily in computer-aided design (CAD) technology to reduce production time and improve quality substantially.

No Silver Bullets for Marketing Success

"Other than sweating the details to create the best value, there isn't one silver bullet to our new product marketing success," says Schmitt. "A large part of it is our history. It's always been an expectation here that new products are vital. They're the lifeblood of our business. It's only through new product growth that we can create opportunities within the company, job security and opportunities for learning."

All of the nearly ten thousand employees of Rubbermaid keep an ear to the ground for trends that could lead to a new product. The business teams, however, drive the new product introductions. A group product manager typically heads a twelve- to fifteen-member team that includes a product development manager, a manufacturing manager, a market research analyst, a finance manager, and a research and development engineer. "They form the nucleus of the team," says Schmitt. "And on an as-needed basis they can pull in any other functions or areas of expertise that they need, either from within the company or outside. In the company's larger units, such as the Housewares Products Division or toy maker Little Tikes Company, there may be as many as seven or eight new product teams at work. In a smaller unit like the Rubbermaid Office Products Group there may be only one or two teams at work."

NEW PRODUCT SWAT TEAMS

While Rubbermaid has large, formidable competitors like Tupperware in the housewares area and Fisher-Price and Hasbro in the toys area, Schmitt says the lion's share of the competition comes from smaller companies that often use a copying strategy to match Rubbermaid. "That's why we needed to find an organizational structure that was equally nimble, so we formed small groups of people that were highly focused, very intense and had a sense of ownership and pride about their project." Rubbermaid now has the advantages of a small organization, yet can leverage the full resources of the company. Rubbermaid literally gets the best of both worlds.

The new product teams aren't formed merely to channel ideas to Rubbermaid brass. "We give the new product teams a lot of authority. The decisions don't just sit around," Schmitt explains. "We don't have a lot of wasted motion where people are preparing things for reviews and scheduling meetings. We try to take all that time out of the process."

WORKING WITHOUT A NET

The fortunes of a new product–driven company such as Rubbermaid obviously hinge on the business teams' success at spotting a trend. An example of Rubbermaid's superb responsiveness to a trend is given below. Rubbermaid sends teams all over the world to hunt for trends. Rubbermaid operates on the premise that it must identify trends. First, they validate them to be sure they are real. Then Rubbermaid researches them carefully to understand fully not just the obvious but the subtleties of the trends—what they mean in both growth opportunities and threats to its growth. "We've come to the conclusion after many years that we've never met a trend that we didn't like," Schmitt proclaims. Banking on trends, especially for a company that doesn't test market, can be risky business. So they do a better job up front of carefully developing the product and validating that it meets the needs of the consumer. Today, Rubbermaid hits the mark with nine out of ten new products. That's a pretty good batting average.

DOING THE GREEN THING

The launch of Rubbermaid's litterless lunch box in 1991 has been one of the company's most successful new product rollouts. In less than a year, the environmentally sound lunch box captured more than 12 percent of the $35 million lunch box market. The litterless lunch box, known as the Sidekick, has been a pet project of Schmitt. He believes strongly that environmentalism will play a leading role in the company's marketing in the 1990s. "We're very interested in the trend toward environmentalism, or green marketing. On the surface, it's a trend that's potentially threatening to a company like Rubbermaid, which makes rubber and plastic products. But when you take a deeper look, it's really a negative trend for companies that make disposable products. We make long-lasting, highly durable products, much of it with recycled plastic. We are creating a demand for recycled material. On top of that, we are able to design a lot of products that make it possible for homes and businesses to recycle plastics and other materials. We're in the catbird seat as we're perceived as part of the environmental solution rather than the problem."

SERVING A LITTERLESS LUNCH

The litterless lunch box found its inspiration in Canada where the government mandated a litterless lunch once a week. It was obvious that litterless lunching was no fad. Everywhere people not only are concerned about eating healthier but are concerned about what they or their children are throwing away, such as juice boxes, paper bags, and plastic sandwich wrappings. By the fall of 1990, engineers in Rubbermaid's Specialty Products Division were basing their design of the litterless lunch box on its existing line of insulated, plastic coolers—the company's existing line of Servin' Saver plastic containers would hold the sandwiches, fruit, snacks, and drinks instead of plastic or paper wrapping.

In January 1991, a Rubbermaid product development team had the prototype of the four-quart lunch box ready. Although the Sidekick was larger than the average lunch box, Rubbermaid was certain consumers wouldn't mind because of its stylish design and striking colors, not to mention the good things it held in store for the environment. This determination proved to be right on the money, but in the meantime there were other considerations. The Sidekick was prepared for late spring production so it could be on retailers' shelves in time for the back-to-school selling season.

Targeting the Right Markets

"We gave a lot of thought to distribution," recalls Schmitt. "We wanted to have the product where people are most often shopping. So we didn't just aim at the mass markets like the department stores but supermarkets and drugstores as well. From a merchandising standpoint, the product was a hit because of its nestability, which allows retailers to stack the product, making optimum use of shelf space."

The product got an unexpected boost by the news coverage of the introduction of the first litterfree lunch box, which generated tremendous positive publicity not only for the product but for Rubbermaid itself. It was a fine example of trend analysis, quality engineering, and marketing savvy.

Rubbermaid also built awareness for the new product through television and print ads, both by itself and in conjunction with its retailers. Rubbermaid's own advertising is primarily brand driven, whereas the ads it produces in conjunction with its retailers focus more on promotions, such as discounts. Rubbermaid's estimated $30 million advertising account is handled by DDB Needham Worldwide's Chicago office.

A Brand That Commands a Premium Price

Underscoring the strength of its brand name in its advertising helps Rubbermaid command a premium price as the Sidekick shows. Although most children's lunch boxes were retailing between $5 and $7, the Rubbermaid lunch box retails between $8 and $10. "From a profit point of view, that price allowed us, as well as our retailers, to get a fine margin. And the consumer was also getting a superb value. There was no resistance to the higher price of our product. The consumer may be able to buy a cheaper product that looks like Rubbermaid or Little Tikes, but if they consider the quality, what it cost us to make it, the level of service we provide, and its timeliness to the market, [the copy] won't measure up."

The price would have been even higher if Rubbermaid did not already have the line of Servin' Saver containers. "It's another example of how we can leverage an existing product line." The premium price also allowed the product development team to reach its goal of a 12 to 14 percent return on the assets invested to develop a new product.

Letters, We Get Letters

How does Rubbermaid know if its products are delighting consumers? "We get mash notes. We get thousands and thousands of letters every month," Schmitt remarks. "We measure the letters—both the good and the bad—very tightly. We listen very attentively to our various audiences." Rubbermaid is so intent on listening to what customers have to say, for example, that it molds a toll-free number into all of its Little Tikes toys to encourage inquiries and suggestions from children, parents, and grandparents. The company epitomizes the relationship marketer that lets the customer call the shots—in sharp contrast to the "We make, you take" mass-marketing mentality of the fifties, sixties, and seventies. That's why Rubbermaid regards every call and letter as an opportunity.

Rubbermaid, however, doesn't worry over every letter from a consumer who wasn't happy with one of their products. "A fair amount of our correspondence about a product where there is some type of problem turns out to be a competitive product, a look-alike. We mold our label into every product, but sometimes people don't pick up on it."

Rubbermaid cleverly turns such misdirected letters into marketing opportunities. "Our Consumer Services Division will contact that person and say, 'You've made a mistake and we understand how you could have made it. Please have a Rubbermaid product on us for free so you'll understand the value of a great product.' We get more terrifically good reaction from that. People like a company that deals with their problem, even if it's not the right company. That's unique and people are delighted by that." Schmitt might have added that this tactic is the essence of adaptability.

> *In our judgment, TV is not the value to the consumer that it was a couple of years ago. The TV market has become splintered. You've lost your target audience. Consumers have so many channels to watch now, we can't find them.*
>
> —DON TYSON,
> FOUNDER, CHAIRMAN, AND CEO OF TYSON FOODS

Tyson Foods has taken brand extension to a new dimension. It started with breaded chicken portions and soon spread to prepackaged chunks and patties. Now the Springfield, Arkansas, producer fixes chicken three thousand different ways.

The world's leading poultry producer runs a fully integrated operation, nudging its flock through every phase of the production process—from first cheep to final shipping. Tyson has its own hatcheries and its own feed mills, it operates sixty-three processing plants, and brings twenty-six million chickens to market every week.

In all of American industry, there may be no manufacturer more dominant in its market niche than Tyson. In fact, Tyson recently bought out its closest rival, Holly Farms, in a $1.5 billion hostile takeover. The acquisition brought Tyson's annual sales up to about $4 billion. Tyson is a major supplier to supermarkets, restaurants, school lunch rooms, institutions, and corporate cafeterias—nearly everywhere, in fact, where chicken is served. The company does business with 80 percent of the nation's fast-food restaurants.

Despite the company's runaway success, however, founder Don Tyson is still hungry for more. "I want 100 percent," he says. "When I get there, the boys can talk to me about something else."

WHICH CAME FIRST?

Don Tyson is a fifth-generation farmer. "My daddy started raising chickens more than fifty years ago," says Tyson. When the younger Tyson became involved in the operation, the biggest problem he faced was the constant fluctuation in the price of chickens. "The problem wasn't raising the chickens," he recalls, "it was trying to sell them at prices that seemed to vary every day or every hour." That's when Tyson stumbled on what he calls "further processed value-enhanced poultry."

His first value-enhanced product was a Rock Cornish game hen that he sold whole—per hen, rather than per pound. "We could sell them at the same price for three or four months at a time," recalls Tyson. "That helped us take the swing out of the commodities side of the poultry business."

Next, he began selling a breaded chicken that was packaged by the portion—and again, he was able to price it by the piece instead of the pound. "That started us thinking: If we can do that with a couple of products, let's see if we can't do it with some more. In 1970, we found out we could sell chicken by taking meat off the bone and making chicken patties or chicken chunks for the fast-food people."

A THOUSAND WAYS TO FIX A PATTY

The chicken patties and chunks (or nuggets) were to become Tyson's first great success in brand extension.

Tyson realized that what worked for the fast-food industry might work just as well for consumers. He began marketing his chunks and patties to supermarkets, where sales quickly flourished. "The fast-food people had already done the market introduction and market advertising of the product for us," says Tyson. Since then, Tyson Foods has built its business on brand extension. "Let the dog have pups," says Tyson Foods president Leland Tollett. "Once we have a winner, we ask ourselves what else we can do with it." Adds Tyson: "We'll take something simple like a chicken patty, and make the finest one we can make and price it accordingly. Then we'll make one that's competitively priced, then we make one that is lower priced for different groups of customers." Typically, the company will introduce a new product in one market—like the fast-food chains—and then reintroduce it into the supermarkets and institutional food service markets (schools, hospitals, and corporations). But before it ever gets to the first market, the product must pass the Tyson test. The company develops and tests dozens of variations in-house—but only a fraction ever make it as far as the focus groups.

"We made a patty for a customer once with a thousand variations in the spice level, the salt and pepper level, and the combinations thereof," Tyson remembers. "But I couldn't sell him on a single one of them. When we got to a thousand variations, he quit me."

With every new product, Tyson tests the widest possible range of seasonings. "You put upper limits and lower limits on all the seasonings—you decide what's too salty or not salty enough. And as you mix in the other ingredients—pepper, garlic, onion—you change the perception of the saltiness, and try to home in on what the consumer wants."

Once Tyson's product developers have a taste they're satisfied with, they test it on consumer groups from several parts of the country. Company researchers typically spend a day with a focus group, dishing out samples and asking questions. "We find out, 'what do you like about it, what don't you like about it, would you buy this, what price would you pay for it?'" says Tyson. "We're always looking at pricing points. It has to be a value for the consumer or the consumer will reject it."

THE PRICE IS RIGHT

As in all businesses, proper pricing is a key to success in the chicken business, but an affordable price without the quality is a sure road to failure, Tyson insists. Experience has taught him that the customer will rate the product on quality rather than price. "If you start selling on price alone your quality will suffer. The customer recognizes poor quality. They want to get it as cheap as they can, but if it's too cheap, they'll stop buying it."

The trick is delivering quality while maintaining low prices. "Go with quality over price, and then make sure you're a low-price producer. As long as you are the low-price producer, your competitor will have to lower the quality to underprice you. When they start lowering the quality, the customer will know it."

Selling the Supermarkets

With the constant battle for shelf space, getting new products into supermarkets can be a very tough sell. Tyson's reputation and past success in the market gives the company a decided edge, but it's no guarantee of success. Before going national with any of its new products, Tyson first tests the product with focus groups, then tests it in a handful of selected stores, and often introduces it on a regional basis. If the product succeeds at every level, the company will push it into the national market.

"We go in and say, 'We've done enough market research to project that this product will move at this volume at this much margin, and it's better than some of the products you're selling. It will make you this much money per foot of shelf space.' That's what you have to convince them of."

Once a grocer agrees to stock a product, Tyson must back it up with enough marketing punch to keep the product moving. One chain Tyson sells to has a flat-out policy that if sales fall below $800 per week, they discontinue the product. With today's sophisticated computerized scanning systems, retailers can track sales by the week, by the day, and even by the hour.

A Chicken a Day

The typical market life of a successful chicken product is two to five years, but many will die long before that. That's why Tyson tries to put new products on the market almost every day. Generating new products is all part of the company's brand extension strategy. "For example," says Tyson, "we make twenty-six varieties of patties. Out of that twenty-six varieties, we probably have five to eight different spice levels and five to eight different breadings. We also may put them out in different sizes and shapes—round, square, oblong, heart-shaped, you name it. We have to do that because every customer,

every restaurant, wants its own personal patty in its own area. Those are called signature products."

That's why the chicken sandwich at Hardee's tastes a little different from the chicken sandwich at McDonald's and the chicken sandwich at Burger King and the chicken sandwich at Wendy's—even though they might all be supplied by Tyson Foods.

Product turnover in the restaurant market tends to be much faster than it is in the grocery business. Restaurants may change chicken products every few months just to give customers a new taste. "Whatever they want we're going to try to have it for them," says Tyson. "Most of the new products you see were tested six months to a year before they make it onto the menu."

GETTING THE MESSAGE OUT

Tyson spends $50 million a year for marketing, but unlike many of the other food giants such as Kellogg and Quaker Oats, you won't see many Tyson commercials on television.

"In our judgment, TV is not the value to the consumer that it was a couple of years ago," says Tyson. "The TV market has become splintered. You've lost your target audience. Consumers have so many channels to watch now, we can't find them." As a result, the company has shifted its advertising focus to print media and radio. With radio, Tyson hits customers as they're driving home from work—exactly when they are most likely to do their shopping.

With print media, Tyson prefers advertising in the upscale magazines that may carry recipes and gourmet features, such as *Good Housekeeping, Better Homes and Gardens,* and some regional magazines.

SELLING THE SCHOOLS

Tyson supplies chicken for many of the nation's largest school systems, including New York, Chicago, Los Angeles, and San Francisco. In the highly competitive school lunch market, the greatest difficulty is convincing the schools to switch from a product they have been serving to a new product Tyson is offering.

To persuade a school system to buy its products, Tyson must:

- Show administrators that they meet nutritional requirements.

- Show that they fit well within the lunch room budget.

- Show that the kids will eat them—after all, the students probably already eat Tyson products in restaurants and at home.

But the proof of the pudding, as they say, is still in the eating. Tyson prepares a sample meal for schools to give students a chance to try out the product. "If we can show that the kids like it, that it's good for them, and that it's competitively priced, then all that's left to do is to ask for the order."

Define your unique niche and stick to it, keep your powder dry financially, take advantage of the opportunities when they come but not to the point that you're overextended when the bad times come, and stay flexible.

—DAVID RIDLEY,
MARKETING DIRECTOR OF SOUTHWEST AIRLINES COMPANY

Gravity isn't the only force the airlines have to defy to stay aloft. Rising fuel prices, fluctuating passenger loads, tight margins, and brutal competition have grounded a growing list of airlines.

Only one carrier, in fact, has managed to turn a profit every year since 1973. Although Southwest Air may not be one of the nation's three or four largest airlines, it is certainly one of the most successful.

The Dallas-based carrier has become an ace of the airline industry, strangely enough, by competing with the car.

"That is a fundamental tenet of designing a short-haul (less than five-hundred-mile) trip—to make airline travel so affordable that you get people out of the car," explains Southwest marketing director David Ridley. Southwest has turned Texas into one big city. It has more than seventy daily flights between Dallas and Houston at a cost—depending on when you book the flight—of as little as $68 per round trip! It has also expanded into several other south-western states, the Midwest, and established a growing presence in California.

IDENTIFYING NEW ROUTES

Southwest's strategy for evaluating new routes is finding markets that are overpriced and underserved. In identifying potential new routes, the company examines several elements:

1. What is the current demand for airline service between those cities?

2. What is the regional business tie between those two cities?

3. What is the volume of highway travel between those two cities?

"When we enter a market, it is not a matter of saying the amount of air traffic between this market is X, so we're going to get our share of X," Ridley explains. "What we say is, the total amount of traffic between two cities is currently X, but because we will reduce the fares so much, we will induce more air travel. We'll have more business travelers, and we'll make leisure travel so affordable, we'll compete with the backyard barbecue. You'll decide to go ahead and go see Aunt Alice for a weekend trip that you wouldn't have taken otherwise because you didn't want to spend seven hours in the car."

When Southwest began offering service between Dallas and Little Rock, the airline volume was about one hundred thousand passengers a year. "Three years later, after Southwest entered the market, it was up to four hundred thousand passengers a year," says Ridley. "That was because of the added stimulus of lower air fares."

Typically, when Southwest enters a market, it sets its fares at about one-third of the existing rates charged by the other airlines serving that market. When Southwest added flights between San Diego and Burbank and between San Diego and Sacramento, the standard walk-up fare was $279 one way. "We entered the market at $59, everyday, no strings attached, and if you wanted to buy advanced purchase, it would be less than that," says Ridley.

The market responded quickly. People who would never have considered flying from Sacramento to San Diego for the weekend—at

$279 each way—or the business person who had a possible deal in San Diego but had to think twice about the $600 in air fare were suddenly lining up to buy their round-trip tickets at just $118 a pop. Southwest also offered ten to fifteen flights a day, enabling business travelers to fly out in the morning, meet their contact, and return to the office in the afternoon. "The other advantage of offering all those flights each day," Ridley notes, "is that if your meeting runs late and you miss your flight, you don't have to wait four hours for the next flight. You only have to wait forty-five minutes to an hour for the next Southwest flight."

KEEPING COSTS DOWN

How can Southwest afford to offer air service at one-third to one-fifth the cost of other carriers—and still make a profit?

"It boils down to simplicity of operations," says Ridley. The savings come in several forms.

ONE TYPE OF AIRCRAFT

Southwest uses Boeing 737s for all of its flights, which reduces dramatically the training time for its pilots, flight attendants, and mechanics. Stocking parts and inventory and training mechanics to work on an array of aircraft—as the other airlines must do—is very costly.

MORE EFFICIENT GATE USE

Most airlines fly a hub-and-spoke system. Flights tend to arrive in waves to make it more convenient for passengers with connecting flights. When the wave of flights departs, "there's about a two-hour hiatus during which those gates aren't used," says Ridley. "But the airline is still paying rent on those gates."

Southwest Airlines doesn't use a hub-and-spoke system. They have no connecting flights, nor do they need them because of the frequency of the flights they offer to each city they serve. Instead, Southwest uses a point-by-point system. Its planes may fly from Dallas to Lubbock to Albuquerque to Phoenix to San Diego, keeping its gates occupied and its employees busy on a nearly continuous basis—unlike the major carriers, which may use their gates only seven or eight times a day.

FASTER TURNAROUND

Because Southwest does not operate on a hub-and-spoke system, it can dramatically reduce the time span between arrival and departure. Southwest turns its aircraft around in fifteen to twenty minutes, compared with an average turnaround time for other carriers of about forty minutes.

"Airlines only make money when they're in the air," says Ridley. "They don't make any money sitting on the ground. This is an asset utilization game. Our point-by-point system allows us to keep our planes in the air longer."

LESS PAPERWORK, FEWER EXPENSES

Seating is offered on a first come, first served basis on Southwest flights, enabling the company to eliminate the time and effort other carriers put into reservations and seat assignments. Nor does Southwest offer meals on any of its flights, which also adds to the savings. Southwest concentrates on the one-hour to one-and-a-half-hour trips in which meals and assigned seats are less of a priority.

USE OF SECONDARY OR ALTERNATIVE AIRPORTS WHEN POSSIBLE

Rather than fly out of the major international airports, Southwest operates out of the less-expensive secondary airports of the major cities. In Dallas, for instance, it flies out of the downtown-based Love Field rather than Dallas-Fort Worth International Airport.

Selling the Service

It doesn't take a lot of effort for Southwest to get the word out on its low fares and frequent flights. When a carrier can come into a market at a fare one-third to one-fifth the cost of existing carriers, word spreads very quickly. But Southwest still does its share of advertising. "We try to club them over the head with everyday low fares and high frequency," says Ridley. "We're trying to maintain the loyalty, the quality of service, and remind people of our frequency of flights." In Texas, the company serves ten major cities and carries 70 percent of the passenger load on flights within the Lone Star state. "You're an hour away from any city in Texas," states Ridley. Southwest's slogan: We've made Texas one great city.

An earlier ad slogan was this: Southwest, the company plane.

"The idea was that we're as convenient and accessible as the company plane," adds Ridley. "Whenever you want to go, we're there. We have hundreds of stories in our files of people who have built their businesses around us."

On to California

When Southwest entered the California market, the company played on the memories of the now defunct Pacific Southwest Airlines, on which Southwest Air was modeled. "They were known for their high frequency, no gimmicks, no advanced purchase, very friendly personnel," Ridley recalls. "They even had smiles painted on the front of every plane. Unfortunately, the company was purchased in the late 1970s by USAir, which painted over the smiles, raised the fares, and ultimately walked away from 70 to 80 percent of its intrastate business. When USAir pulled out, we jumped into the void."

Southwest's brilliant advertising theme was "Happy Days Are Here Again." Its commercials showed cartoon caricatures of the old happy face planes (easily recognizable as the Pacific Southwest fleet) being gobbled up—to the *Jaws* theme song—by a fleet of huge, monstrous planes (a thinly veiled reference to USAir). Then, to the tune of "Happy Days Are Here Again," the voice-over said, "But Californians, Southwest Airlines is proud to announce new service between San Diego and Oakland (or other routes), returning low fares and lots of flights. Happy days are here again!"

"There was an instant connection because we were identifying with the fond recollections of what California residents had lost." Within six months, Southwest had become the leading carrier out of San Diego, Oakland, and Burbank.

Beating the Odds

In an industry that has seen the demise of one carrier after another— People Express, Braniff, Eastern, and Midway, among others—Southwest has managed to thrive by sticking very closely to its core philosophy. "Define your unique niche and stick to it, keep your powder dry financially, take advantage of the opportunities when they come, but not to the point that you're overextended when the bad times come, and stay flexible," says Ridley. "We are tempted all the time to alter our service. All the time, we hear, 'Why don't you fly to Mexico—there's a lot of business there' or 'Why don't you add a little nineteen- or thirty-passenger feeder flight into Chicago Midway from Moline and Peoria.' That's a distraction. That's not who we are."

People Express, which initially modeled its service after Southwest, was very successful in its early days. "Then they decided they wanted to fly four-hour flights, transcontinental, long-haul flights, even to London. They lost sight of who they were trying to be. Midway Airlines did the same thing," adds Ridley. "They were doing okay flying out of Chicago, but then they decided they needed a hub in Philadelphia. But when the Iraqi crisis hit and fuel prices spiked, they were overextended and overleveraged. They had survived for twelve years in this business and if they had just stuck to their knitting, they would still be doing okay. But they wanted to be something other than what they were." The opportunities for expansion are abundant for Southwest. In 1991, the company was petitioned by thirty-three cities who wanted the carrier to introduce service in their airports.

"But sometimes," says Ridley, "the best strategy is to do nothing. To his credit, our chairman, Herb Kelleher, has resisted all that. Fundamental to all this has been his absolute obsession with fiscal conservatism. He understands that there is one absolute truism in the airline business, which is, there are going to be bad times. It is an incredibly cyclical industry. His overriding philosophy is to manage in the good times like it's the bad times."

This simple policy has kept the good times flying at Southwest Air.

People really don't buy computer technology based on need—they buy it based on emotion.

—MEL MASTERS,
PRESIDENT AND CEO OF LASERMASTER TECHNOLOGY

LaserMaster Technology is known for its high-performance laser printers and add-on enhancement cards. What really fueled the company's rapid ascent, however, was its ability to spot problems and engineer solutions long before anyone else even recognized the problem.

"What we've tried to do all along is find niches within the laser printer arena that were not being properly served by the bigger players," says Mel Masters.

The company's first product in 1986 was an add-on controller card for the IBM PC that enhanced the performance of Hewlett-Packard LaserJets. "The HP LaserJet could do three hundred dots per inch resolution, and it could do full-page printing," says Masters. "The problem was it couldn't do them both at the same time. It could do full-page printing, but at a very low resolution. We came up with a way to combine both things and made it do what people wanted it to—high-resolution and full-page printing." It's that knack for ironing out glitches in the laser printer market that propelled LaserMaster from $1.5 million in sales in 1988 to $56 million by 1991. But the laser printer market—like all phases of the computer industry—has become fiercely competitive. LaserMaster is one of dozens of emerging computer-related companies whose earnings have suffered the past two years as a result of intense pricing pressures. The company has tried to stay a step ahead of the market by concentrating heavily on research and development. It maintains one of the world's largest printer driver development groups with eighty-five engineers.

"We're always looking over the horizon to figure out where the market is heading," says Masters. "The key focal point for us is, What are the application guys doing? In the computer business it doesn't matter what the hardware guys are doing, what matters is what software application is hot. What are people buying? What does it do that people would want it to do better? And then we go in and try to fix those problems."

WINDOWS OF OPPORTUNITY

LaserMaster's most recent window of opportunity has been the Microsoft *Windows* application that has become almost standard fare for new computer buyers. *Windows* software is selling at the rate of about one unit every four seconds. And every time a new *Windows* package is sold to a laser printer user, LaserMaster gains another prospect. According to Masters, *Windows* slows the printing capability of many laser printers from about forty-five seconds per page under DOS to about eight minutes per page under *Windows*. "With our printers," Masters says with a smile, "it takes six to twelve seconds. We had the first hot printer solution for *Windows* on the market (as of 1992). We were twenty to thirty times faster than everybody else on the market. We worked for almost two years on optimizing the *Windows* printing process while the rest of the printer manufacturers in the world have just now awakened to the fact that it's a problem. So unless they license technology from us, it will be two years before they can pull it off. We have a two-year head start on the market."

FINDING ITS MARKET

Developing problem solving technology is only half the battle. The other challenge is finding the specific computer users who need that technology. *Windows* users may know they have problems with their laser printers, but they may not know there's a way to fix those problems. Reaching those people takes some well-targeted marketing.

LaserMaster attacks the market from several fronts:

- *Direct-mail marketing.* "If we could do only one thing, it would be direct marketing. That's the most effective tool in our business," says Masters. The company sends out about 250,000 mailers per month to targeted groups of laser printer users.

- *Trade journal advertising.* The company promotes its key products in *PC Magazine* and other computer-user periodicals.

- *Trade shows.* "I don't think we sell much through trade shows, but we get a lot of credibility because we send primarily engineering people," says Masters. "You've got all these users out there who really enjoy being able to talk to our technical people about the nuances of the products."

- *Public relations and trade journal articles.* Masters considers PR and trade journal placements the least important form of marketing for LaserMaster's high-end products. "PR is more relevant when you're doing mass marketing for commodity products. It's less relevant when you're doing target marketing for high-performance niche products like ours."

DEALING WITH DEALERS

LaserMaster markets its wares primarily through mail order and through some three hundred certified publishing consultants who are specialists in the business printing market. "You can buy an HP laser printer at any department store. To buy our product, you have to go to a specialist who understands the software applications and knows why it's going to be to your advantage to buy a high-performance mechanism." In addition to the three hundred specialty dealers, LaserMaster has sales agreements with another five thousand dealers—although most of them don't stock any LaserMaster products. "But if someone walks in and orders a LaserMaster," says Masters, "they know where to order it, and we can ship it out that day."

Like most smaller manufacturers, LaserMaster has met with its share of frustration getting dealers to keep its products in stock. That's why the crux of the company's marketing is aimed at consumers. "You can't sell anything to dealers," says Masters. "If dealers don't have a place to move it, they're not going to buy it. So it doesn't do me any good to try to sell the dealers. That's why we don't try to push things into the channel. We go around the channel and create a demand from the user."

Masters outlines the typical scenario: "A customer walks into a store, slaps down one of our ads and a MasterCard, and says, 'Do you carry LaserMaster?' The dealer says, 'Certainly,' and goes to the back room and calls us on the phone, and says 'Hey, how soon can you get me XYZ?' That's far more effective than us calling that guy up for months trying to get him on-line as a dealer. So we do his job for him."

PRICING

LaserMaster shoots for a 44 to 47 percent gross profit margin on its products, although that figure can vacillate—either way—depending on the competition.

Because its printers tend to be higher performance than the mass-market printers, LaserMaster can charge more, but not too much more. It's a delicate balance.

MARKET RESEARCH

LaserMaster is constantly in touch with its customers to come up with new products and product refinements. But the company shies away from market research in the traditional sense—it does no formal statistics gathering and conducts no focus groups.

Instead, the company turns to two other sources to gauge customer reaction.

1. *Telephone sales.* "We monitor our sales presentations very closely," says Masters. "We know what customers are telling us and what they're asking for."

2. *Trade shows.* The trade shows can help in a couple of ways—as an information-gathering source for the engineers and as a proving ground for the company's new products. The company sends three or four of its newest innovations to demonstrate at the shows. "We'll show them all in the booth, and then we watch people's reactions," says Masters. "People really don't buy computer technology based on need—they buy it based on emotion. We look at their eyes, we look at their body language, we see what they react to. And that's our market research. You can hire consultants to go out and gather statistics all day, but I'd trade one trade show for all those statistics."

We've been blessed with the mouse. It's brought us to where we are today. In a sense, though, it was like flying a plane with only a single engine. You couldn't afford to make any mistakes. But with our broader product line, there's more room to maneuver.

—PIERLUIGI ZAPPACOSTA,
PRESIDENT AND CEO OF LOGITECH

Logitech knows that the PC mouse is essentially a commodity product—any manufacturer can make one and plenty of them do. Competition in the $300 million worldwide market is fierce and getting fiercer as the pointing devices increasingly become standard equipment on personal computers.

At the retail level, Logitech locks horns with the high-tech titan Microsoft and in the big-stakes original equipment manufacturer (OEM) market competes against a host of smaller computer peripherals makers. Logitech's OEM customers include IBM, Apple, Unisys, and Hewlett-Packard.

But Logitech is winning the mouse wars. The Northern California–based company has sold more than ten million mice, capturing nearly 40 percent of the global market for the popular high-tech items. At the retail level, Logitech has succeeded with its so-called Swatch strategy, explained below.

SEGMENTING THE MOUSE MARKET

"We can make a mouse for nearly every taste," explains Pierluigi Zappacosta, the company's Italian-born president and CEO who allows that Logitech stole a page from the marketing playbook of Swatch, the flamboyant Swiss watchmaker. "Anyone can build a mouse. We build them differently."

Do they ever. For children, there's the Kidz Mouse, which features two buttons that look like ears, a pointed nose, and a pair of simulated eyes. For southpaws, there's a left-handed mouse. For the ham-fisted, there's an extralarge mouse. There are even cordless radio mice. If there's a unique segment at the retail level for a mouse, Logitech will fill it. Logitech can't take credit for developing the mouse—a product created in 1965—but it was the first company successfully to market the device that's become a standard appendage to the personal computer.

Slightly more than half the mice the company makes are destined for retail markets such as computer dealers and computer superstores where the strategy of offering several product line extensions plays especially well. About 45 percent of the mice are produced for the OEMs, which incorporate the mouse into their own products. Sales and earnings at the $230 million company have been growing more than 30 percent a year.

Fabio Righi, the company's vice president of marketing, says the line extension strategy wasn't designed to impress its OEM customers. They're looking for more than that. "With the OEMs, we've struck strategic alliances to ensure they're getting exactly what they want from us. Our salespeople have very strong relationships with them. That's been a strong channel of distribution for us—both domestically and internationally." Righi says about 55 percent of the company's sales are in the United States, 35 percent are in Europe, and the remainder in Asia and other parts of the world.

Founded in 1981, Logitech got to most of the key OEMs ahead of the pack and worked harder than the competition to keep them satisfied. The company supplies mice to more OEMs than any other manufacturer in the world.

To bring a product to market, Logitech forms interdisciplinary teams that include representatives from marketing, manufacturing, quality control, and product support. For example, for MouseMan, Logitech created two separate teams—one in its Fremont, California, headquarters and the other in its European headquarters in Romane/Morges, Switzerland—each sensitive to what would sell on their respective continents. They worked in tandem to establish a successful worldwide marketing strategy.

During the product's sixteen-month development, the trans-Atlantic teams communicated frequently over the phone or through e-mail, but when the logistics became too daunting, members of one team would fly to the other's workplace to meet in person.

MARKETING BEYOND THE MOUSE

But as fascinating and successful as Logitech has been, Zappacosta wants the company to be known as more than the world's leading pointing device maker. "We've been blessed with the mouse," Zappacosta admits. "It's brought us to where we are today. But with a broader product line we can now set our sights on more ambitious goals." Logitech achieved a sort of critical mass in 1988 thanks to the mouse and continued to ride that product's success through 1991.

"In a sense, though, it was like flying a plane with only a single engine. You couldn't afford to make many mistakes. But with our broader product line, there's more room to maneuver," explains Zappacosta. "I'm surprised how far we've come in ten years. Life is full of wonderful breaks. If I had not come to study at Stanford I would have never met the other people who started this company." While earning his graduate degree in engineering at Stanford, Zappacosta met the future Logitech chairman Daniel Borel, then a graduate student. Borel, along with Zappacosta and Righi, launched the company built on the humble computer mouse.

Zappacosta believes the mouse and the hand-held scanner have helped humanize the otherwise impersonal personal computer. "We think of the mouse as the hands of the computer and the scanner as the eyes of the computer." He would still like to humanize the computer further. To do so, however, he'll have to do nothing short of re-creating the company he co-founded in 1981. "In a crowded field, it's important for the marketplace to attach some image to your name," Zappacosta explains.

INSTILLING A SENSE OF MISSION

For its next step, the company is repositioning itself to be known as the "Senseware" company to underscore the point that Logitech can help personal computer users to bring a more intuitive, human feel to their machines. The company is halfway there already with its pointing, imaging, and scanning devices. But Zappacosta wants to take an even more intuitive approach to personal computing by adding a new type of software that will bring genuine ease of use to the computing world.

Zappacosta will not elaborate on these new products, but he will say that he wants every employee in the company pulling in the same direction as the company redirects its flight path. To this end, Zappacosta is meeting with as many of the company's 350 employees as he can. For example, he held a four-hour meeting with the company managers, sales force, and marketing department to lay out his vision of the company's future.

"It's not an easy process. Every employee, not just sales and marketing people, must have this shared sense of religion," proclaims Zappacosta, who's taken his message to the company's offices and manufacturing facilities around the world. "In some cases, I've met with twenty to thirty employees in the cafeteria for a few hours or with employees on the manufacturing floor. I'm hoping to answer the employees who come to me and ask, 'Where are we going next?'" Zappacosta's evangelistic mission is designed to instill employees with a stronger sense of purpose and a laserlike focus on the company's new strategy. To establish Logitech in the marketplace as the

Senseware company, Righi says the company is convening a conference to introduce the concept and the products Logitech offers to support Senseware. Logitech customers, prospects, and influential people in the computer hardware and software fields will be invited to get a firsthand look at the company's new direction and products. "We'll have a good story to tell," boasts Righi, with justification. He regrets that the company's profile in the marketplace has been too low key. "The company's image is that of a creator and manufacturer of unique products that are beautifully designed and engineered, but the company lacks a particular personality."

To boost the company's image, Righi says the company began television advertising in 1991 and has advertised in leading computer trade magazines to the tune of about $2.5 million a year. The company continues its emphasis on customer service.

Logitech maintains a customer service hot line and a technical support hot line and invites customers to tap into its seven-day-a-week, twenty-four-hour electronic bulletin board. The company also has recently launched its innovative FaxBack in which a Logitech computer automatically faxes technical support information to customers requesting information. "What our customers say about us to others is critical to our success so we need to do better," says Righi. "The harder we work at it, the more realize how much there is to do."

THE SUREST PATH TO
YOUR CUSTOMER'S HEART

BUILDING CUSTOMER LOYALTY—and the repeat business that comes with it—takes more than quality products and clever advertising. It takes a commitment to step beyond the expected. Don't just satisfy—surprise, excite, and delight. The great companies have learned that the more you put into your customers, the more you get out of them.

"We don't want to simply meet our customers' needs," says Stanhome, Inc. chairman H. L. Tower. "What we strive to do is surpass their expectations." For its giftware customers, Stanhome sponsors annual and regional conventions, offers tours of its manufacturing facilities, and sends out a monthly full-color newsletter to half a million collectors to keep them abreast of new products.

Other companies have come up with their own ways of giving customers extra value for their dollar. Gerber offers a toll-free hot line, twenty-four hours a day, 365 days a year, for parents who might have questions on the care and feeding of their young children. Pitney Bowes gives customers a five-year full guarantee on its office equipment. If you're not satisfied at any point in the first five years, Pitney will deliver a free replacement; if you're still not satisfied, the company will give you a 100 percent refund.

You can go out and academically study the market and draw some conclusions about what your customers want, but at a certain point you need a sanity check on all your assumptions.

—KATHLEEN E. SYNNOTT,
VICE PRESIDENT OF WORLDWIDE MARKETING
FOR THE MAILING SYSTEMS DIVISION OF
PITNEY BOWES, INC.

Few companies would complain about its flagship product commanding an 88 percent share of a $2 billion market. But Pitney Bowes, the world's largest maker of postage meters and mailing equipment, once controlled 99 percent of the U.S. meter market. That was until three European competitors invaded the U.S. market in the 1960s and spent the following twenty-five years chipping away at the market leader.

In the mid-1980s, Pitney Bowes, realizing it was technologically vulnerable, made the conversion from manufacturer of simple mailing machines to producer of high-tech "smart" mailing systems that could electronically presort, fold, insert, and stamp pieces of mail. "There was a perception both internally and externally that Pitney Bowes was in a mature industry and that we really weren't going to be able to grow our business," explains Kathleen Synnott, Pitney's vice president of worldwide marketing of the Mailing Systems Division. Rather than watch its grip on the mailing systems market grow even weaker and its earnings flatter, Pitney Bowes took several key steps to shore up its position. The company has:

- Invested more than $500 million in new technology in the past five years.

- Launched the most significant new product cycle in its history, featuring products that could be marketed on a global basis.

- Announced and implemented the above-noted customer service guarantee program.

- Redoubled efforts to strike closer relations between its 1.3 million customers and its sales force by training its reps to serve more as consultants than salespeople.

Pitney's intensive research and development drive began filling its new product pipeline in 1990, unfortunately, just as the national economy was slipping into a recession. Despite the economic climate, Synnott states, "We wanted to give our customers a reason to do business with us. New products are one way to get their attention."

REGISTERING GOOD RETURNS

The returns on Pitney Bowes' investment in new technologies and marketing look promising for the $3.3 billion company, which reported a 12 percent increase in net income in 1991. The Stamford, Connecticut–based company, which also markets copiers, fax machines, and voice-processing equipment, serves nearly every large- and mid-size company in the United States. In 1991, Pitney's Mailing Systems Division's sales were $1.8 billion, accounting for 54 percent of the company's revenues.

Over the years, the company has been accused of being a monopoly because of its lock on the postage-meter business. The company, founded in 1920, has always maintained a hand-in-glove relationship with the U.S. Postal Service, which is well aware of the criticism directed at Pitney. But the Postal Service is also well aware of the efficiency Pitney's 1.2 million meters have brought to corporate mail rooms, which in turn help the Postal Service save about $500 million a year in operating costs. Customers don't seem to mind either, because Pitney mailing systems, such as those that presort and/or bar code postage, can save them 10 to 20 percent a year on postage costs.

Pitney Bowes has other time- and money-saving devices as well. "Our Postage-by-Phone system, for example, sharply reduces traffic in the front lobbies of post offices," says Synnott, who explains that the fourteen-year-old metering system allows corporate customers to refill their postage over the phone lines rather than hauling the postage meters to a post office to be reset. About half of Pitney's customers have a Postage-by-Phone system, which in 1991 produced about $5 billion in postage.

THE NEW PRODUCT PIPELINE

Thanks to the enormous investment in technology, Pitney has many new and innovative products to sell to corporations desperately seeking ways to trim their mailing costs. Some of Pitney's largest corporate customers spend close to $100 million a year on postage and are obviously receptive to systems that can control their back-office expenses.

The company's Mail Center 2000 series of mailing systems will command a premium in the marketplace, because there are no comparable competitive products. The Mail Center 2000 series of products can perform such functions as automatically reading addresses against a data base to ensure accuracy and help a company manage its mailing costs as well as addressing letters from personal computers. Despite rising postal costs, more companies are using direct mail to better target customers and prospective customers. For example, Pitney has developed a special software product to let customers create and manage high-quality bar-coded address lists to take advantage of postal discounts. Pitney, in essence, reinvented itself. It's no longer in the postage business but in the mailing business.

SELLING THE NEW TECHNOLOGY

All the new whiz-bang products are great, but Pitney's customers are looking for much more than technology, says Synnott. "From a marketing perspective, what's important is that these new systems are offering a solution to the customer. They're asking for help on how to apply technology and for service. It's the understanding of the application that you provide though your sales organization."

And Pitney has just the thing to deliver the solutions—the Mailing Systems Division's seven-thousand-member sales and service force. (About three thousand are sales reps, twenty-three hundred are service reps, and seventeen hundred are sales administration and support.) Unlike many marketers of office-supply products that distribute through networks of dealers, distributors, or agents, Pitney Bowes sells its products through its own sales force, allowing it complete control of distribution.

"One of our key differentiators and our greatest strength is our direct sales," explains Synnott. "We have a formal sales training program that everyone must go through that includes product knowledge, leasing options, and the latest on postal regulations. The training emphasizes relationship selling. That is, the salespeople are taught not only about a product's technology but how the product can be applied to a customer."

A FEEL FOR THE CUSTOMER

Pitney's customers receive more personalized sales and service. In turn, Pitney gets a more intuitive feel for its customers, something that would be difficult if it relied on an outside, independent sales force. Pitney also gains a competitive edge through "segmenting," the careful study of its customers' interests, awareness levels, and buying patterns. "We segment our customers by letter volume and postage volume," Synnott explains. "We segment them by the type of equipment they use. And we segment our customer base on whether they buy or lease their equipment."

Armed with that analysis of its customers' patterns, Pitney can better target its marketing messages, fine-tune its sales tactics, learn which benefits appeal to which customers, and zero in on the key decision makers at a company.

DIRECT RESPONSE

"We have a very strong direct-response marketing effort," explains Synnott. "We make about twenty-two million customer contacts a year through a combination of direct mail and telemarketing." Customer or prospective customer names are supplied by the company's three thousand sales reps and supplemented by outside lists of corporate decision makers that the company buys from list brokers, according to Synnott. The sales leads developed through direct response, trade shows, and publicity are designed to shorten Pitney's sales cycle.

The company's current corporate ad campaign underscores Pitney's service by way of customer testimonials, a technique advertising experts believe is the best way a company can credibly deliver a message to its target audience. One ad, for example, features Edward Meyers, manager of University of California at Los Angeles's (UCLA's) Mail Services who says, "When I joined UCLA Mail Services, our equipment was obsolete, employees were demoralized and managers were frustrated. And I was faced with the job of handling forty-two million pieces of mail a year. So something had to be done right away. I called Pitney Bowes and they went right to work. They had new mailing machines installed and our people trained in no time. Today, we process double the volume of outgoing mail as in the past." The print ads appear in such national business publications as *The Wall Street Journal, Fortune, Newsweek,* and *Business Week.*

Unlike its sales and service force, which is dispersed geographically, the direct-response unit is centralized in Trumbull, Connecticut. The company, however, is considering integrating its sales force with its direct-response forces at the district level. "The advantage is better control," says Synnott. "Sometimes when you have more than one sales channel you have conflict. We're experimenting with concepts that would allow us to become more integrated." As part of this potential combination, the direct-response unit's primary goal is to develop sales leads for the company's field reps, and it has begun selling entry-level metering systems through the mail and over the telephone, according to Synnott.

A Dose of Reality

To keep its perspective fresh on what its customers want from them, Pitney's sales force forms what it calls *reality commissions.* "You can go out and academically study the market and draw some conclusions about what your customers want, but at a certain point you need a sanity check on all your assumptions," states Synnott. Small groups of sales reps, sales engineers, and leasing agents form the ad hoc committees that help give the company a better feel for what its customer wants. Reality checks are also provided by focus group of customers, used extensively by the company's quality-customer satisfaction group.

Or Your Money Back

Since 1990, Pitney Bowes has been putting its money where its mouth is. That's when the company announced its Customer Satisfaction Guarantee.

The warrantee states,

This five-year guarantee means that if you are not satisfied with the performance of this product, Pitney Bowes will promptly replace it at our expense. If we provide a replacement product and it does not fully perform according to specifications, we will promptly give you a full refund. You will have no concerns after you acquire this product. Our customer satisfaction guarantee means that your problems are our problems and will be resolved promptly. In short, it means no excuses from Pitney Bowes.

The guarantee "really formalized the unwritten rule at Pitney Bowes that we stand behind anything we've sold or serviced for five years," says Synnott. "I firmly believe that the guarantee has made a significant change in the culture at Pitney Bowes."

To send this signal to the sales force, Pitney Bowes is offering bonuses to its sales force for meeting or exceeding customer satisfaction targets. Customer satisfaction standards have been established in each of the company's market segments. Some of the things Pitney is measuring include how well they trained the customer's operator, how well they installed the machine, and how well they provide after-sale support. Pitney pays very close attention to the customer's satisfaction with the product's features and its pricing. Customers are asked to rate Pitney's performance on a seven-point scale and are also asked such questions as "What is the likelihood that you would recommend Pitney Bowes?" and "How likely would you be to buy again from Pitney Bowes?"

"We have high customer satisfaction. Almost 94 percent of our customers are satisfied," boasts Synnott, who notes that figure is based on quarterly customer surveys. "We'll continue to measure customer satisfaction in a number of different ways. It's embedded into the objectives of the company in terms of all our performance. But what we're really looking for are 'very' satisfied customers, and that's the range we're trying to move toward."

Getting from the "satisfied" to "very satisfied" level impels the company to focus on areas of dissatisfaction. Several cross-disciplinary teams are scouring the customer base to determine where Pitney Bowes may be falling short.

PENETRATING INTERNATIONAL MARKETS

Pitney Bowes has been selling its wares internationally since 1929, but its new line of products will provide it a firmer grip on overseas markets, says Synnott. About 27 percent of the company's revenues are from exports, a figure that will continue to grow because the company's new products can be more easily adapted by international customers. The company's products had been primarily designed to North American standards, but Pitney Bowes will be taking the marketing battle to the strongholds of its three leading European competitors—Postalia GmbH of Germany, France's Alcatel N.V., and IMS/Hasler, a unit of the Swiss concern, Ascom Holdings.

Although Pitney Bowes is a very familiar name in American and Canadian mail rooms, the company lacks that same recognition internationally. They are advertising more internationally in addition to meeting with each of the country management teams to plan their strategy in each specific market. Pitney Bowes sells in about 120 countries.

Overseas, the company uses a combination of its own sales force along with a network of dealers and distributors. In some Asian countries, Pitney Bowes sells through joint ventures.

PITNEY'S SUCCESS FORMULA

Regardless of where Pitney is peddling its wares, Synnott says the same sales and marketing formula is applied. "We make our mark through superior after-sale support, customer support, ongoing technical support, as well as information about changes in our product line and changes in postal regulations. If acquiring a particular piece of equipment is a problem we can tailor a solution to a customer's financing needs as well.

"Our greatest strategic advantage is our large base of 1.3 million customers," says Synnott, who notes the company has taken full advantage of the customer base by first of all learning what it wants and then delivering the appropriate product backed by intensive levels of service.

I don't want to compare our curtain rods with the competition, I don't want to get into item-by-item price comparisons. What we tell the customer is that

in ten feet of display space, we're going to make more
money for you than the other guy.

DANIEL C. FERGUSON, CEO OF NEWELL COMPANY

Over the past two decades, the Newell Company has established itself as one of the nation's leading housewares manufacturers by thinking big—and thinking small.

This Freeport, Illinois, operation sells over $1 billion a year in household goods. Over the past five years, Newell has posted annual earnings and revenue gains of about 25 percent. It has achieved that success by:

1. Targeting only the largest-volume retailers.

2. Sticking with the most basic product lines.

"We stay away from the high-fashion stuff," says Newell CEO Daniel C. Ferguson. "We're in drapery hardware [curtain rods], but not in drapery. We're in paint applicators [brushes and rollers] but we're not in wallpapers. There's fashion in curtains; there's no fashion in curtain rods." By sticking with the basics, Newell keeps its product line management simple and its development costs to a minimum. "Current rods have a product life cycle of fifteen years; drapery may have a life cycle of six months to two years."

"We're not into the Hula-Hoop seasonal stuff, either," adds Ferguson. "Our products are on the market twelve months a year. That way, our operations are consistent, the predictability is much easier, and we can run on a much more planned basis."

The other key strategy that has contributed to Newell's outstanding growth has been its unwavering focus on a single retail segment: large-volume retailers. "We don't chase specialty shops. We don't chase gift shops. We're strictly in the Kmarts and the Wal-Marts—the big discount chains. We're in Target—not in Dayton's. Today, five thousand discount stores handle the same volume that two hundred thousand stores would have handled years ago."

FOCUS ON PROFITABILITY

Newell is not the only player in the staple volume housewares business. The company must constantly battle competitors who may have newer lines or better prices. Newell's successful and unorthodox marketing strategy in building its customer base has been to stress bigger profits—not lower prices. "I don't want to compare our curtain rods with the competition, I don't want to get into item-by-item price comparisons, I don't want to compare the weight and color of our curtain rod with another item," says Ferguson. "What we tell the customer is that in ten feet of display space, we're going to make more money for you than the other guy. We're selling that total drapery hardware program. That has to do with the display, the color of it, where the various items are positioned on the display. That's all preplanned. That's been our expertise since day one."

The firm has helped retailers boost sales of its more expensive products by giving them preferred placement in the display. "Typically, a retailer may put his $1 paintbrushes right at eye level, but you can't find the $5 brush that makes all the money. We reverse all that. In our layout, you can hardly find the $1 brush, but the $5 brush is right there at eye level. We direct their eye to the more expensive item. We've had a lot of success stories where we've changed the profitability of a chain that let us merchandise the department for them. Whereas most of their sales had been in the 'good' or 'cheap' end of the line, when we get done, most of their sales are in the 'better' or 'best' end of the line."

On-time delivery is another important component of Newell's marketing strategy. The company boasts an on-time delivery record (within two to three days of the order) of nearly 99 percent. "I've run into companies with eight- to ten-week delivery backlogs," says Ferguson. "That can cost the retailer 5 to 35 percent of his profit from being out of stock. So the first thing the retailer is after is consistent in-stock possession. Anybody can make this stuff. Our strength is merchandising it correctly, getting it to the store on time, keeping it in stock, and displaying it correctly—that's the service we perform for our retailers."

LIMITING THE PRODUCT LINE

Ferguson is constantly approached with proposals to add new products, but with rare exceptions, Newell resists the temptation to expand its offerings.

"People are always trying to get me into more product lines. I don't want any more if I can help it. It's too hard to control. If I've got $1 million to invest, the number one priority would be to invest it in an extension of a product line we're already in rather than a brand new product area. If I can get further into cookware in the mass volume, I'll go there. But if somebody wanted to get me into water sprinklers, I wouldn't be interested. Someone once suggested we get into paint sprayers. Our answer to that was to stick with manual items. When you get into electric sprayers, you're no longer selling a $5 item, you're selling a $100 item. And you don't sell it the traditional way, you sell it on promotions and give-aways. It's an entirely different business than the bread-and-butter business we're in."

While simplicity is a key to Newell's success, the company will act on a good opportunity that fits into its overall corporate scheme. One example is the company's recent entrée into the office-products market. With the rapid growth of home offices, the retail market for office products has exploded. As sales volume picked up, the discount stores became increasingly interested. And as their interest mounted, so did Newell's.

The office-products category has become one of the top six departments in Kmart. Sales have been moving quickly from the mom-and-pop office products stores into the mass merchandisers. To capitalize on the trend, Newell recently acquired three growing office-products manufacturers, Sanford (the marker manufacturer), Keene Manufacturing, and W. T. Rogers Company.

Because Newell already had a strong sales relationship with the discounters through its other products, the transition into the office-products market was a relatively easy one.

Despite its exceptional growth, Newell does almost no advertising to promote its products. The only exceptions are its well-known Anchor Hocking and Vise-Grip lines, which rely on advertising to maintain a presence in the market.

"Our business is what we call 'push,' not 'pull.' We push it into Kmart whereas Procter & Gamble pulls it out of Kmart through all of its advertising. We know there's a market for paint applicators, but no one is asking for our brand. In fact, if Target wants its own brand on it to call it the 'Target Paintbrush,' we'll make it that way."

KEEPING THE EDGE

Adaptability has always played an important role in Newell's marketing strategy—and the future should be no different. "We need to be more flexible than ever. We're dealing with some chains that want to go to warehousing, others that want to drop it; some that want private brands, others that want national brands; some that want in-store service, some that don't; some that want preticketing, some that don't. The manufacturer needs a policy of flexibility that allows him to tailor a program to the needs of each retailer."

Ferguson also sees a couple of other trends in retailing that manufacturers will have to adapt to: better buyers and fewer vendors. Retailers are hiring better trained, better educated, and more sophisticated buyers. Manufacturers need to respond by hiring better trained, better educated sales executives.

To reduce red tape and paperwork, retailers are cutting back on the number of manufacturers they buy from. Ferguson contends that manufacturers need to adapt by offering a more complete product line. "If they need only one source, make sure that source is you."

We try to measure everything we do in terms of "Does it really surprise and delight our customers beyond their expectations?" If it does, we're doing our job. If not—if we only meet their expectations—we haven't gone far enough.

—H. L. TOWER, CHAIRMAN OF STANHOME, INC.

When Gene Freedman added the Precious Moments porcelain collection to his Enesco line of giftware in 1978, it was with no special marketing thrust—"no great fanfare," as Freedman recalls.

But in the weeks that followed, Freedman began to get the sense that the forlorn cherub-faced children he had helped create were striking an alluring chord in the hearts of middle America. The reaction was like nothing he had seen in his more than twenty years of peddling giftware. "You could sense a special aura about these fig-urines, an enthusiasm," Freedman recalls fondly. Enesco started get-ting calls from customers. Stores began selling out of certain lines. Demand soon became greater than supply.

Since those early days Freedman has helped shape the Precious Moments collection into a national cultural phenomenon. More than six hundred thousand Americans are members of the Precious Moments Collectors Club, and millions more are avid buyers. Pre-cious Moments is the number one collectibles line in the world, earn-ing Enesco sales revenue of more than $100 million a year.

The success of Precious Moments has helped make the sixty-six-year-old Freedman wealthy beyond his wildest dreams. Nonetheless, the "self-proclaimed protector of Precious Moments" continues to pursue a grueling schedule: meeting with presidential aides at the White House to unveil a new Precious Moments figure honoring America's servicemen, shooting an Easter Seals video spot with Pat Boone, signing autographs for the hundreds of busloads of collectors who make the pilgrimage to his suburban Chicago office each year, and traveling to the Far East to coordinate manufacturing operations or open new production facilities.

"I cherish the success," says Freedman with a sigh, "but there is no euphoria." A gracious, devoutly religious man whose conversa-tion is sprinkled with "Thank the Lord," Freedman admits that the collection's success has been for him both a blessing and a curse. "I agonize every day," he says. "It's a responsibility to half a million collectors, it's a responsibility to ten thousand retailers. People have to believe in you. They have to believe that Gene Freedman is not going to do anything to taint the Precious Moments collection."

Freedman first came up with the idea for the Precious Moments collection in 1978 after seeing some inspirational greeting cards that featured the somber kids with the teardrop eyes. He contracted with the artists, Sam Butcher and Bill Biel, to produce a series of similar drawings that could be converted to porcelain figurines at Enesco's production facilities in Japan.

Over the next several months, the team put together a line of sev-enteen Precious Moments figurines. The figures were distributed along with Enesco's other lines of giftware to specialty and depart-ment stores throughout the United States.

TIGHTENING THE CONTROLS

As the popularity of the Precious Moments collection grew, it became increasingly evident to Freedman that Enesco would not be able to meet the demand. Ordinarily, high demand and low supply is the kind of headache most manufacturers love. But while most managers would have solved the shortage by increasing supply, Enesco contracted instead of expanding. Freedman tightened the reigns on distribution, cut out the wholesalers and set maximum limits for the retailers.

It wasn't a popular decision within Enesco. "I must admit," recalls Freedman. "I had a lot of differences with my staff. But we finally decided to bite the bullet." It was a bullet that turned to gold. The controlled supply increased the value of the pieces and transformed Precious Moments from standard giftware to sought-after collectibles, which appreciated rapidly. For example, a figurine of a girl and a puppy that sold for $12 in 1981 now commands $2,000.

Over time, Freedman weaved together a promotional and marketing strategy that has helped preserve the value of the Precious Moments pieces while sustaining a growing market. The strategy aims at both customers and retailers in a variety of innovative ways.

To accommodate avid collectors, Freedman established a Precious Moments collectors club. "We were bombarded by questions about the figurines and the artist and so forth. We realized we needed to start a Precious Moments collectors club that could answer all the questions, create excitement, have events in stores, etc." To promote the club, Enesco included membership forms along with each figurine that was sold in the stores. Freedman anticipated membership of about five thousand collectors. Instead, membership swelled to sixty thousand the very first year.

Club members receive a quarterly glossy color magazine called *Good News Letter* with profiles on club members, updates on new Precious Moments figures, and other related news. Members also get an opportunity to buy two "members-only" figurines a year that are not available to the general public. The members-only figures cost more than most Precious Moments pieces, but because of the limited availability, they often double or triple in value within two to three years.

A recent members-only piece cost more than $300 and was expected to sell twenty thousand to forty thousand pieces.

Enesco hosts an annual national convention and several regional conventions to promote the collection and bring collectors together. Freedman and artist Sam Butcher traditionally speak at the annual convention, sign autographs, and charge up the troops.

Along with the national club for collectors, the company helped establish a nationwide network of local clubs. There are now more than five hundred clubs. Enesco has also started several other collectors clubs for its other products.

Collectors are also invited to visit the Precious Moments Chapel. You could call it the Graceland of Precious Moments—although true believers prefer to refer to it as their Sistine Chapel. More than four hundred thousand collectors a year visit the Precious Moments Chapel in Carthage, Missouri, where Precious Moments children depict biblical stories and Christ's life in fifty-four giant murals and fifteen stained-glass windows, all painted by Precious Moments artist Sam Butcher.

Promotions alone, however, won't put the product in the customer's hands. To support the Precious Moments line at the retail level, Enesco pursues a variety of tactics.

Of the ten thousand retailers who are allotted Precious Moments pieces, one thousand stores are designated as "Distinguished Service Retailers." "In order to qualify, they must carry all the Precious Moments figurines, advertise, hold special events, and really live up to what the collection stands for," states Freedman. As part of the Distinguished Service Retailers program, the company maintains a staff of retail event directors to stage special events for collectors. The events typically draw anywhere from a few dozen to a few hundred collectors and may include slides of future introductions, special videos of the production process, and other features. "It's all designed to excite the collectors." The company also offers a training program for retailers to teach them how to sell collectibles—both the Precious Moments figures and the other newer lines of collectible items produced by Enesco. Freedman continues to explore other avenues of marketing, including direct mail, but he is proceeding cautiously. "The idea is not to sell as many Precious Moments figurines as you can. The idea is to maintain the integrity of the collection. We have to walk a very fine line."

BEYOND EXPECTATIONS

Stanhome, Enesco's corporate parent, has set the goal of doubling sales and earnings every five years. But rapid growth can sometimes take a toll on the level of quality and services a company offers. Stanhome chairman H. L. Tower insists that won't be a problem.

"We don't want to simply meet our customers' needs. We try to measure everything we do in terms of 'Does it really surprise and delight them beyond their expectations?' If it does, we're doing our job. If not—if we only meet their expectations—we haven't gone far enough.

"That's how we've built Precious Moments into the leading collectible in the world," adds Tower, "and that's how we are achieving our corporate objective of doubling our sales and earnings every five years."

A successful business must have intimate contact with the marketplace. In our case, we must educate the surgeons on the use of our products. They receive a lot of information. The most important thing is the technical backup and the innovative technology.

—DANE MILLER, PRESIDENT AND CEO OF BIOMET, INC.

Biomet makes implants for joints such as the hip, knee, and shoulder. Dane Miller sometimes wonders if the company is marketing to its target audience of orthopedic surgeons or simply educating them. Biomet is really doing a little bit of both very well. The fifteen-year-old company, based in the small northern Indiana town of Warsaw, has been racking up 30 percent increases in sales and profits on an annual basis.

Miller would like to think that Biomet's educational approach has played a large role in the $275 million company's success. "I've seen a big shift in how products are marketed in the orthopedics device industry from simply selling to genuinely educating the customer." Biomet realizes it can't match the marketing might of such

Fortune 500 pharmaceutical giants as Bristol-Myers Squibb and Pfizer, each of which have industry-dominating orthopedic divisions. But because it's smaller, Biomet can do things better than the market leaders and eat away at their share of the market.

STRIKING CLOSE RELATIONS

Miller cites Biomet's Patient-Matched Implant program as an example of how the company works hand in glove with orthopedic surgeons. By using information from a patient's computed tomography scan (CT scan) or through magnetic resonance imaging (MRI), Biomet re-creates three-dimensional models that the surgeon can use to prepare for a difficult or unique reconstructive surgery. On short notice, the model is translated into a design for the custom implant. Even though the program doesn't make much money directly for Biomet, it's well worth the effort because of the bond it creates between orthopedic surgeons and the company.

Dane Miller founded Biomet along with three other young entrepreneurs with a $500,000 loan from the Small Business Administration. The loan has long since been repaid, Miller points out with entrepreneurial pride. Fifteen years after its founding, Biomet finds itself demographically well positioned to serve an aging population, which will increasingly need what it makes.

HOSTING ITS TARGET AUDIENCE

Another way the company builds relations with orthopedic surgeons is through a tour program that brings more than four hundred surgeons to the company's headquarters each year. Key surgeons from around the country are identified by Biomet's sales representatives and then booked for a trip to the Hoosier State. "The program gives our sales people some time with the doctor away from the distractions of the hospital and office. And the surgeons have the opportunity to meet our management, engineers and product managers," explains Joel P. Pratt, Biomet's vice president of sales and marketing, who adds that the company uses the tour to underscore its computerized design and manufacturing capabilities.

The surgeons are flown in the day before the tour and treated to a meal that evening. The next day, a small group of surgeons gets a tour of the plant and a comprehensive education on Biomet's product line. The program teaches the surgeons the intricacies of a Biomet design.

In addition, surgeons are invited to leading hospitals around the United States to observe reconstructive procedures involving Biomet products. They're also enrolled in Biomet-sponsored seminars where surgeons describe how they use the company's products. "It's all part of our effort to convince the marketplace," Pratt says.

THE CRITICAL LINK TO SURGEONS

The critical link between Biomet and the U.S. orthopedic surgeon community is the company's network of 240 independent commissioned sales representatives and sales associates. Biomet's distribution network extends overseas where its products are sold in more than one hundred countries. About a quarter of Biomet's sales are international and the company expects that figure to grow throughout the 1990s. Biomet has invested heavily in its sales network through intensive training and commissions that are the envy of the industry. New Biomet sales representatives are put through eight weeks of training at its Warsaw headquarters, and veteran sales reps' skills are sharpened through week-long training sessions.

Key to Biomet's marketing is adapting its products and delivery of them to the exacting requirements of its surgeon/customers and their patients. To learn what they want, Biomet has worked to create an atmosphere where they can learn what their market wants, be it on one of the company's jets, during a plant tour, or over a quiet dinner in a restaurant near the company's headquarters.

"We're always looking for the best way possible to hear what our surgeons have to say," says Pratt.

It's pretty clear: The more direct contact you have with your customer, the easier it becomes to build your brand franchise.

—STEVE POOLE,
DIRECTOR OF PUBLIC RELATIONS FOR
GERBER PRODUCTS COMPANY

Businesses have turned increasingly to toll-free numbers to facilitate sales and compile prospect lists. But Gerber takes a different tack with its 800 service. The baby food producer gets more than half a million calls a year on its toll-free lines—without making a single sale.

"In fact," says Steve Poole, Gerber's director of public relations, "we generally don't even get the names and addresses of the people who call."

Gerber's 800 line serves parents with questions. The Fremont, Michigan, producer began its toll-free service in 1986 with eleven operators. (The 800 number was printed on all of Gerber's products and later was included in many of its ads.) In its first month the company received fifteen hundred calls. Now the company gets almost fifty thousand calls per month.

As successful as the program has been, it would seem to be a natural source of excellent leads for further direct-marketing sales efforts. But Gerber doesn't see it that way.

"Certainly that has been discussed," says Poole, "But our main concern is to provide answers for those mothers. They're looking to us for help—not to be bombarded with other information from us. The only names and addresses we capture are those who want more information or follow-up. We are very careful not to use the names for promotions, nor do we sell the names to other companies. We see it as a sacred trust," he adds. "We feel that the relationship between the consumer and our operators is something not to be misused."

More important than collecting those names is building brand loyalty. A distressed parent who can call Gerber toll free at three o'clock in the morning to answer his or her questions is probably going to be a loyal Gerber customer for as long as there are little ones at home to feed. The strategy is pretty clear: The more direct contact you have with your customer, the easier it becomes to build your brand franchise. There are about four million births a year in the United States. The six hundred thousand calls Gerber receives each year represent a good percentage of those babies.

The two questions parents ask most:

• When should our child start solid foods?

• What food should we start with?

INTO THE FUTURE

Gerber has a long tradition of consumer education. As early as the 1930s, Dorothy Gerber was actively involved in answering letters from parents and wrote a regular newspaper column in which she addressed many of the most-asked questions.

By the mid-1980s, the company was getting about five thousand letters a year from parents, but Gerber suspected that there were a lot of other parents with questions who couldn't take the time to write. Like all great companies, Gerber found a way to adapt to meet the changing needs of its customers. "There were societal changes that dictated that we had to have an 800 number," says Poole. "We recognized that there was a much greater pent-up demand for information than we could provide by answering letters."

In 1991, the company extended the service to twenty-four hours a day, seven days a week. For working parents, nine to five on weekdays was not a very convenient time. Gerber now receives calls throughout the evening and well into the night. As we all know, babies don't keep regular hours.

"In fact," adds Poole, "we even get calls on Christmas Day. People say, 'I can't believe you're there,' but they're always very grateful. That's what you call franchise building."

An anecdote from a young father who called the service illustrates its widespread respect. "We were at our pediatrician's office to discuss how we should start feeding our infant," said the father, "and the doctor was suddenly called out on an emergency. As he was racing out the door, he scribbled the Gerber 800 number on a piece of paper, handed it to us, and said, 'Here, call Gerber, they'll answer all your questions.'"

RELATED BENEFITS

Brand loyalty is not the only benefit the call-in service provides. There are some other indirect benefits as well.

SHOPPER ASSISTANCE

Gerber fields a lot of calls from people who can't find specific products such as nursing pads. The Gerber operators can usually give callers the name of a store in their area that carries the item.

NEW IDEAS

Gerber credits calls from customers as a key reason the firm began offering baby food in more convenient smaller jars.

QUALITY CONTROL

"We use the toll-free line as an early warning system for any problems we might have," says Poole. "If the consistency isn't right on a batch of peaches, for instance, or there's an off-taste, we can identify the batch from the open date coding and feed the information to quality control. They might find that they used a different brand of peaches for that batch and decide, based on those call-ins, not to use that brand again. That type of thing happens almost every month."

WINNING THE CONSUMER WARS

THEY ARE WHAT EVERY CONSUMER WANTS, and every smart marketer tries to deliver: value and convenience. Consumer-oriented firms that offer the best of both are the ones that stand to prosper in the 1990s.

At McDonald's, marketing vice president David Green says value can mean more than just the price of a Big Mac. "There's more to McDonald's than the food. It's the experience and the feeling that you get when you go to McDonald's. That's a very important part of our success."

At Oshkosh B'Gosh, the added value has always been in the quality and durability of its clothing. In fact, boasts president and CEO Douglas Hyde with justifiable pride, the company's toddler-wear "was, quite frankly, overconstructed for children. But that was part of the mystique . . . our garment was different, it was better made, it was more expensive, it could be handed down from child to child to child and not wear out."

Kinder-Care likes to offer a little bit extra, like staying open until nine P.M. at least one night a week to give parents a chance to go to dinner, run errands, or just take a break.

In the retail business, value is just part of the picture. Convenience can be equally important. Walgreen's entire operation is predicated largely on shopper convenience—convenience in the broad product selection offered in its stores, convenience in its round-the-clock hours, and convenience in the location and easy accessibility of every outlet.

Convenience is so important to Subway founder Fred DeLuca, in fact, that he coined his own strategy for staking out the most convenient locations for new Subway shops: PVA. "That's people, visibility, and accessibility."

In some businesses, though, there is no substitute for advertising. No one is more aware of that than Zeos International CEO Greg Herrick, who places as many as twenty pages of full-color ads in a single *PC Magazine* issue to tout his Zeos personal computers.

Aveda founder Horst Rechelbacher prefers a more evangelistic approach. To spread the word on his line of natural shampoos and personal care products, Rechelbacher travels the country hosting styling seminars for hair care professionals. He also touts his products at his internationally renowned styling school in Minneapolis.

It takes three elements—value, convenience, and effective marketing—to succeed in the highly competitive consumer market of the 1990s.

It's apple pie and motherhood, but success of a retail operation is defined as three things: location, location, location. We believe in that.

—VERNON A. BRUNNER, EXECUTIVE VICE PRESIDENT
OF MARKETING AT WALGREEN COMPANY

We don't want to just be on the right street, we've got to be on the right side of the street.

—LAURIE MEYER, MANAGER OF CORPORATE
COMMUNICATIONS AT WALGREEN COMPANY

There is nothing quite like a walk through Walgreen's. It is retail bursting at the seams; long, snug aisles teeming with an eclectic array of odds and ends, gifts and gadgets—alarm clocks, school supplies, trash cans, house slippers, eyeliner, potato chips, plants, toys, tapes, jewelry, art work, and twelve-packs of pop.

Disparate as it may seem, however, the company's shotgun approach to merchandising can be tied neatly together in a single word: *convenience.*

"We appeal to an awful lot of age brackets, young, old, male, female, married, you name it," says Walgreen marketing chief Vernon A. Brunner. "We find that from a consumer point of view *convenience* is the key word." From its product mix to its twenty-four-hour-a-day operations to its strategically selected store locations to its satellite-linked network of pharmacies, Walgreen has made convenience the focus of nearly every marketing initiative.

The formula works. Walgreen has quietly become one of America's steadiest and most profitable retail performers. Recessions pass it by; the company has posted seventeen consecutive years of increased profits. With seventeen hundred stores in twenty-nine states and annual revenues of $7 billion, Walgreen is the nation's largest drugstore chain.

Walgreen has made it to the top of this fiercely competitive business by leaving nothing to chance. It weighs every detail and monitors every sale. "We manage from a daily, weekly, monthly, yearly basis as to what trends are happening on each individual product we carry," says Brunner.

THE GOODS

Nearly every item in a Walgreen's store could be categorized, to one degree or another, as a "consumable." The term applies not only to foods and medications but also to most of Walgreen's other lines—from batteries and tapes to inexpensive watches, clocks, and radios.

"In a lot of respects, price also relates to the word *consumable,*" says Brunner. "From a convenience point of view, if you break your clock radio and you need a replacement, you have a couple of choices. Are you going to go out and shop for a $50 to $100 clock radio, or are you going to go over to Walgreen's where you can pick up a replacement clock radio for anywhere from $3.99 to $19.99? That to me is a very consumable item."

Walgreen's makes its product selections based in part on market research and in part on instinct or gut feeling, as Brunner puts it. One of the company's more successful new product lines was an assortment of wind-up twin bell alarm clocks that the company decided to offer after monitoring buyer trends. "The trend was up, the novelty aspect was there, the packaging was there, and the gut said let's do it." Sales of the clocks reached about thirty thousand units a year.

Walgreen was also quick to jump on the new Gillette Sensor razor. It was the first chain to stock it. "We pride ourselves on being first if it's a product the customer expects to find in Walgreen's. And we work very closely with the manufacturers to see that that happens." Its early jump on the Sensor razor enabled Walgreen to sell almost 10 percent of Gillette's total first year production. It's all part of the company's strategy: Get the product out there, get it merchandised, support the manufacturer's advertising program, price the product competitively, stay with the product, and ride its introduction to the hilt.

Of course, not every product works quite as well as the Sensor razor. Witness the Tater Twister. Brought to market just in time for the 1991 Christmas season, it looked like a natural to Walgreen's buyers. It could slice, dice, and curl cut a potato in seconds. It seemed the perfect last-minute holiday stocking stuffer. "It was a very cute item," says Brunner. "We thought sales were going to be pretty good, and that the advertising would be there to drive the sale. But none of the above happened. We sold a fair amount, but nowhere near our investment."

Brunner is philosophical about the Tater Twister experience. "When you get into a seasonal selling period, you're taking a risk on a lot of new products. You're always going to make some mistakes."

WHERE TO PUT IT

The back-of-the-store soda fountains and restaurants that were once a trademark of Walgreen's have all disappeared. Their demise was brought on, in part, by "the McDonald's phenomenon," as Walgreen corporate communications manager Laurie Meyer puts it. "The fast-food industry really impacted the in-store restaurant business."

The other key reason for dropping the restaurants was space allocation. The company simply found more profitable ways to use the space, expanding its lines of over-the-counter remedies, vitamins, and other personal care items.

Space allocation is an issue the company reviews and refines almost daily as part of the constant reshuffling and reallotment of products. "New products are the lifeblood of retail," Brunner states.

But for every product it adds, Walgreen must find one to delete. Again, the company counts on trends and gut feelings to make the cuts. Housewares is a prime area the company recently scaled back to make room for the boom in the toiletry and over-the-counter drug markets. At one time Walgreen devoted as much as eighteen to twenty-four feet of shelf space to trash cans, wastebaskets, laundry baskets, and other plastic housewares. Today, Walgreen has reduced the department to just six feet of shelf space, with a basic pail, a basic wastebasket, a small trash can, and one laundry basket. The convenience is still there for customers, but Walgreen can use the additional space for more profitable product lines.

APPLE PIE, MOTHERHOOD, AND LOCATION

Location has always been a primary focus of the retail trade, but no one does it quite like Walgreen. You'll find its stores in the heart of bustling downtown business districts, at key intersections in major suburbs, in the marquee spots of outlying shopping malls. "It's apple pie and motherhood," says Brunner, "but success of a retail operation is defined as three things: location, location, location. We believe in that. We try to control the rent factor, but prime location is very critical to us."

The company spares no effort in ferreting out choice sites for its new stores. Every location is studied for traffic patterns, egress and ingress, population growth, demographics, competition, sales potential, and (here's that word again) convenience. "Convenience is a real key. How visible is it? What about parking? How easily can you get in and out?"

The site selection process begins with a market research committee that studies potential sites and collects information. Next an operations group ponders the financial feasibility, then a real estate group evaluates the site, and finally, the executive committee, including chairman Charles R. Walgreen III and president L. Daniel Jorndt, personally reviews the proposal and casts the deciding yes or no vote.

"A site doesn't get through our committee easily," says Meyer. "We don't want to just be on the right street, we've got to be on the right side of the street."

TECHNOLOGICAL ADVANTAGE

Every Walgreen store in America has a satellite dish that taps it into the nationwide network of stores. The system monitors store-by-store sales and inventory, but Walgreen also uses the system to gain a marketing advantage over the competition. "We made the commitment to technology from a productivity point of view," says Brunner, "but we also tried to turn it around into a marketing concept for the consumer that made us unique in the marketplace." The thrust is that customers can call 1-800-WALGREEN from anywhere in the United States to find the nearest Walgreen and the nearest twenty-four-hour Walgreen. If you need a prescription—and you're registered with Walgreen—you can have your order filled in any Walgreen's store anywhere in the twenty-nine states. In fact, even if you're outside Walgreen market territory, the company can have your prescription delivered to your doorstep overnight. Thus the company's recent advertising slogan: "Anytime, Anyplace." "We've gotten a lot of letters from people who said we saved their vacation," Meyer reports.

The satellite network also has some other benefits:

- The on-line scanning function helps the central warehouse track buying patterns and maintain inventory control.

- Customers looking for a product that may be sold out of one Walgreen's store can track it down instantly at other nearby stores through the network system.

- Important messages (like product recalls) can be transmitted systemwide simultaneously. When the Tylenol tampering case broke in 1982, every store in the Walgreen system was notified instantly through the systemwide linkup and each pulled its stock immediately.

- Product scanning functions can be controlled systemwide from the home office, which means that price changes can be made instantly in all seventeen hundred stores. "Our cashiers used to have one heck of a time remembering what was on sale," explains Meyer. "Consequently there was a high margin of error." Now Walgreen can transmit its advertised prices to its stores instantly.

- The company has the ability to transmit music and in-store announcements to all seventeen hundred stores, and Brunner soon expects to begin testing video transmissions to the stores to provide information for customers on new medical products—both over the counter and prescriptions. The system also offers "bimarket" capabilities. In other words, if it is snowing in Minneapolis and sunny in Florida, Walgreen can run sun tan lotion announcements in Florida and snow brush announcements in Minneapolis—all centrally controlled.

THE FUTURE

Walgreen plans to continue relying on new technology to stay a step ahead of the competition. The company has developed a complex inventory control system dubbed the Strategic Inventory Management System (SIMS) that will facilitate automatic reordering in the stores. The secret to SIMS, says Brunner, is in its forecasting capability. The traditional sell-one-buy-one inventory control strategy provides some benefits, but if it lacks seasonal adjustments, the store is buying based on past rather than future sales. The SIMS system will factor in seasonality and buying trends in its reordering allotments.

It's one more marketing advantage that will keep Walgreen growing well into the next decade.

You must be willing to embrace change and deal with it. I am constantly having to remind myself that this is a new year. Don't assume that because something worked five years ago, it will work again today— because it probably won't.

—DOUGLAS HYDE,
PRESIDENT AND CEO OF OSHKOSH B'GOSH, INC.

Like the tiny preschoolers who don its line of britches, shirts, and skirts, growth came fast and furious for Oshkosh B'Gosh in the 1980s. "Almost everything we touched seemed to turn to gold," recalls Douglas Hyde. Revenues grew steadily from $48 million in 1981 to $315 million in 1991, and net profit climbed tenfold from $3.8 million in 1981 to $38 million in 1989.

Then growing pains began to take a toll on the Wisconsin manufacturer. While revenues continued to edge up, earnings dropped 20 percent in 1990.

To stem the tide, Oshkosh has adopted a more sophisticated marketing approach. "The whole ball game has changed," says Hyde, whose family has managed the business since 1934 and still controls the majority of voting stock. The old-fashioned improvise-as-you-go approach no longer works. As Hyde puts it, "We have to do a lot more homework, really plan our strategies, and then execute them flawlessly if we want things to be successful."

FROM BIBS TO CRIBS

For nearly eighty years—from its inception in 1895 until the late 1970s—Oshkosh B'Gosh had a pretty good fix on its customer base. Its market was the American farmer who wore Oshkosh bib overalls to plow the fields, milk the cows, and feed the hogs.

All that changed in 1978 when Oshkosh discovered an exploding new market. For many years the company had produced a line of children's overalls for a mail-order house. "They were selling six or seven thousand pairs a year. Finally we said, whoa, if they can sell all those, maybe there's something out there."

To test the idea, Oshkosh sent out a direct-mail piece to children's specialty retailers. "The response was phenomenal," recalls Hyde. The company's full stock of children's clothing sold out within a month. "We thought we had enough in stock to last three or four months. That's when we realized that there was really something there."

Now, about 96 percent of the company's sales are generated by its children's clothing.

COUNTRY CHIC

Children's wear was a fertile market in the 1980s, fostered by the new baby boom. And while there was plenty of competition, Oshkosh quickly found its niche.

"We were offering a level of quality that was just unheard of in children's wear back then," recalls Hyde. "Our garment was made just like we make a work-wear garment. It was, quite frankly, over-constructed for children. But that was part of the mystique. Back then children's wear was considered disposable; it was kind of cheap. Our garment was different, it was better made, it was more expensive, it could be handed down from child to child to child and not wear out."

The Oshkosh brand also conveyed a certain charm, or country chic. "Maybe it was reverse snob appeal." The areas where it caught on first were New York, Boston, Los Angeles, and San Francisco, where it was very new and different. As the company's success grew, it added a growing array of new styles and new lines—knit tops, swimsuits, outerwear. And consumers snapped up nearly every item of toddler attire the company threw at the market.

NOT SO GOLDEN

With its line of children's wear flying off the shelves, the company assumed that the next logical market would be apparel for older children and adults, explains Hyde. But the adult lines never got off the ground. "Almost without exception, everything we've done outside of children's wear—men's, women's, maternity, youth wear (older children)—has not done so well," Hyde concedes. Part of the problem was a lack of solid market research. "We didn't do our homework, we didn't have a sound strategy, we didn't understand the dynamics of the market or what we would have to do to compete."

Oshkosh hasn't given up entirely on the adult market. In fact, it now markets lines of men's and women's clothing that are moving, albeit modestly. But the company treads much more cautiously these days in adult attire.

GROWING PAINS

In spite of its failures in adult garments, Oshkosh continued to cruise through the 1980s with a long string of record earnings—thanks to the enormous success of its children's apparel. But over the past couple of years, even the children's line has faced some difficulties. "When 50 to 60 percent of your business is done through department stores—30 percent of which are in bankruptcy, and another 15 percent that are close—you do get a little worried," says Hyde.

The company has adapted to the change in market dynamics by taking several drastic steps. First of all, it changed its retail focus. In 1990, Oshkosh agreed to sell its clothing through Sears and J.C. Penney stores. The decision was not particularly popular with many of the smaller shops that had stocked Oshkosh's apparel for years and considered it an exclusive line. "Some of the retailers now tell us that our line is too widely available. We know we've lost some business because of that, although very few stores have dropped the line entirely. But the net gain of those two [Sears and Penney] has been very, very worthwhile."

Constant change is part of the game in the clothing industry. "The whole issue of keeping ahead of change, understanding it, dealing with it and adapting to it is a key to survival in this business. You must be willing to embrace change and deal with it. I am constantly having to remind myself that this is a new year. Don't assume that because something worked five years ago it will work again today—because it probably won't."

Oshkosh has also been fine-tuning its marketing. It recently hired a top-level marketing specialist and has pursued a series of consumer research projects to gauge the attitudes of both the customers who buy its clothing and the retailers who sell it. "The whole issue of marketing intelligence helps us understand what's going on with the consumer," notes Hyde. "Now that we truly understand what the hot buttons are, we want to make every attempt to point that out to the consumers in a much stronger way than we ever have in the past."

This new marketing intelligence has led to a new ad campaign emphasizing family values. The ads feature scenes from a family at play. One shows a father hiking a football to his young son, another depicts a little girl in her mother's lap painting her fingernails. Oshkosh used real parents with their own children for the photographs, because actors couldn't capture the closeness of the moment—the emotion seemed forced. Using parents with their own kids gave the ads a much more genuine feeling. It captured the image of real clothes for real people. "We're not really selling clothes, we're selling image, we're selling the brand and the feeling in and around the brand."

FURTHER EXPANSION

Oshkosh plans to expand further into the larger retailers. The company is still missing out on the single biggest retail area of children's attire. "The national discounters such as Wal-Mart, Kmart, and Target account for almost 50 percent of the market share in children's clothing," says Hyde. "We need to be represented in that market. Whether it be an acquisition, a license arrangement, or the introduction of a new brand, we feel strongly that we need a vehicle to address the national discount chains."

The discount market, however, could hardly be considered a tailor-made option for Oshkosh. The company's high-end prices would not sell at most discount stores where low prices and high volume are the rule. The company would also risk further alienating its other retailers who have already expressed concern over Oshkosh's decision to sell its line in Sears and Penney. This paradox is not lost on Hyde, who insists that the company will be able to sidestep both potential problems by introducing a different line of clothing—under a different brand name—in the discount market.

One other prime area of further expansion is the international market. "We view international expansion as one of our major growth strategies for 1990," says Hyde. International sales already account for about 7 percent of the company's sales.

We believe the source of creativity is knowledge. To creatively package our learning programs, we need to thoroughly understand our customers. And that takes strong research—not just the obvious questions.

—JOHN KAEGI, SENIOR VICE PRESIDENT OF MARKETING AT
KINDER-CARE LEARNING CENTERS

When 80 percent of your new customers come via word of mouth, you'd better have people saying nice things about you. That's why the marketing effort is anything but child's play at Kinder-Care Learning Centers, the nation's largest chain of child-care centers.

The company figures the best way to grab market share in the service field is to build their service around a distinctive, comprehensive approach to child development. The company's going about it in a number of ways, which are evolving from its focus on professionalism—better teachers, better training, and better retention of teachers. John Kaegi, senior vice president of marketing, elaborates, "Now we're zeroing in on a single theme, which is our Whole Child Development learning program. It's what sets us apart from our competitors' programs that often only consider one element of a child's development. Others simply emphasize their low price."

STAYING ON TOP

Kinder-Care is banking on its multidimensional approach to child development to maintain its position as the biggest name in child care. With its 1,260 centers in forty states and Canada, Kinder-Care has a third of the market share among the chain-operated child-care centers, which include La Petite Academy, Children's World, and Childtime Children's Centers. Although Kinder-Care is the biggest of the chains, it has only about a 1 percent share of the nation's $35 billion a year child-care industry. Nearly three-quarters of the child-care market is considered private, that is parents at home, relatives, or nannies. The small, mom-and-pop–style day-care centers claim about 13 percent share of the market and another 12 percent is controlled by nonprofit institutions such as churches or YMCAs. Kinder-Care and its rival chain-operated centers account for the remaining 3 percent of the market.

DIGGING OUT

Despite the success with its programs, Kinder-Care is digging itself out of a financial morass it slipped into in the late 1980s when its former chief executive Richard J. Greengrass led an ill-fated diversification financed by junk bonds. Financial results are improving as the company reorganizes. It has also spun off such businesses as family portrait photography and life insurance to again concentrate on caring for children. Revenues in 1991 rose to $440 million, 9 percent higher than 1990. As it returns to health, Kinder-Care will embark on an ambitious expansion program and continue to renovate its existing centers. The company has spent more than $35 million in the last two years to upgrade its facilities. Kinder-Care plans to build thirty-five new centers in 1993 and fifty more in 1994.

The company was founded in 1969 by Perry Mendel, who recognized the need for quality care as working mothers fast became the norm rather than the exception. Mendel assembled a group of professionals from the fields of nutrition, early child development, and physical fitness to help create a comprehensive plan for instruction and supervised care. Now, Kinder-Care offers programs designed for age groups from infants—which Kaegi concedes is a loss leader—to twelve-year-olds. Grade-school–aged children, for example, can participate in the Klubmates program, which is provided before and after school and for full days during the summer and school holidays.

PLUMBING THE NEEDS OF ITS TARGET MARKET

As a service provider, Kinder-Care spends a lot of money learning what its customers want. The company devotes more than $150,000 a year to focus-group research. "We believe the source of creativity is knowledge. To creatively package our learning programs, we need to thoroughly understand our customers. And that takes strong research—not just the obvious questions." For example, Kinder-Care learned through its research that younger baby boomers—age thirty-five and under—have sharply different attitudes toward their children than do older baby boomers. "The younger baby boomers are more pragmatic and less idealistic about raising children than their older counterparts, who have more time and money and less guilt," Kaegi explains. "The younger baby boomers, in short, are more stressed out and more receptive to our marketing message."

The company's target market is working, married women between the ages of twenty-five and thirty-nine with household incomes of $40,000 to $80,000 and above-average educational levels. About 13 percent of Kinder-Care customers are working, single mothers, but the company emphasizes working, married mothers in its marketing, because they have far higher disposable incomes.

To reach its target audience, Kinder-Care uses a variety of marketing vehicles in addition to word of mouth or reference selling. To reinforce its reputation, Kinder-Care has recently begun a brand image campaign with the theme: "The Whole Child Is the Whole Idea." Kinder-Care is differentiating itself from the competition by publicizing its comprehensive learning programs. "Our competitors' programs aren't as good as ours. They're canned," says Kaegi.

THE MOST IMPORTANT ADVERTISING VEHICLE

Kinder-Care spent $3 million in 1992 to advertise on drive-time radio. "That's the best time to reach our target audience. When they're either on their way to work or on their way home, they're thinking about their kids." Another $1.5 million was spent on yellow pages advertising, $1 million on direct mail, and $1 million for a print ad campaign. The ads, executed by Dallas ad agency Tracy-Locke, appear in such magazines as *Redbook, McCalls, Working Mother, Working Parent, Parents,* and *Parenting.*

Kinder-Care has not had good results with television advertising. "Working mothers are too busy to watch much TV," Kaegi states. The company, however, is spending about $300,000 in 1992 to sponsor a series of thirty-second public service announcements (PSAs) to talk about child development and how Kinder-Care understands the process.

Kinder-Care also reaches parents with its recently launched quarterly newsletter, titled *Small Talk,* which includes tips and short articles on subjects such as how to return home from work on a happy note, the best way to say good-bye to a child in the morning, and how to help your child overcome stranger anxiety. The eight-page newsletter also addresses such things as the company's policy on sick children, offers book and video recommendations, and includes a survey form inviting parents to rate the service they're getting from Kinder-Care.

PART OF THE FAMILY

Among the things Kinder-Care has learned in its focus-group research is that working mothers lead complicated lives. "They don't all live the nine to five existence. The *Leave It to Beaver* lifestyle is over," Kaegi says. To accommodate the schedules of its working mothers and fathers, Kinder-Care has become more flexible with its own schedule. Most centers will stay open as late as nine P.M. one night a week to allow parents to go to dinner, shop, or pay bills.

Once a month, the centers will stay open as late as ten P.M. on a selected Friday night for a free Kids Night. The real beneficiaries, of course, are the parents. Between 50 and 60 percent of the parents are taking advantage of the extended hours. Some of the centers are also experimenting with weekend hours to give harried, two-income couples and single parents some time away from the kids.

"We want to be a part of the extended family," says Kaegi, "and to do that we must be more accommodating." To ease the end-of-the-day stress for both parent and child, Kinder-Care prepares a hot nutritious snack to tide the youngster over on the way home to dinner. "By the end of the day, the child is not only tired but hungry. Some parents would stop at McDonald's on the way home because the child was so hungry."

IMPRESSIONS ARE EVERYTHING

Research by the company indicated that a child's last impression of his or her day at Kinder-Care is often the most lasting. "If a child ends the day on a happy note that's going to carry over into the evening and the next day. We don't want to send the child home hungry and that makes it easier on the parent," says Kaegi, a father of three. Impressions—first or last—are critical for a company that relies so heavily on word-of-mouth for new business.

The company's focus-group research not only helps Kinder-Care better customize its schedules and learning programs but also provides a forum for the parents to share their concerns over the challenges of parenting. "In essence, we provide the parents a support group, which helps cement the bond between us and the parents. It's a long-term partnership arrangement that builds a community spirit." Parents are provided plenty of feedback from the company's care givers in the form of periodic child progress conferences and written reports designed to keep the parents informed and involved. Parents are encouraged to meet with care givers whenever they feel it necessary and questions are welcomed at the centers that maintain an open-door policy.

STIMULATING CREATIVITY

The centers' classrooms are bright and colorful and designed to stimulate the creative and developmental needs of the child. Kinder-Care's age-specific programs are built on weekly themes, such as seasons, colors, safety, pets, shapes, and sizes. The programs, however, are only as strong as the staff responsible for them, which is why Kinder-Care has increased salaries and benefits of its staff. In an industry that operates on razor-thin margins, providing employees with the leading compensation package has been difficult. Kinder-Care's operating margins have been in the 7 percent range, but the company would like to push it back to 10 percent. The company's net profit margin has been running in the 1 to 3 percent range. To offset the cost of higher salaries and benefits, Kinder-Care had to increase its tuition by 4 percent in 1992.

Despite the rising cost of child care and stagnant population growth, Kinder-Care's research indicates there will be a 4 to 6 percent increase in demand for child-care in the 1990s over the previous decade. Kinder-Care, which has more than one hundred twenty thousand children enrolled in its programs, anticipates a steady expansion through the decade.

CORPORATE OPPORTUNITIES

Employer-sponsored child care holds the greatest promise for Kinder-Care in the 1990s. The company recently established its Kinder-Care at Work Division, which creates a child-care center or takes over an existing center for an employer. As Kaegi sees it, "A lot of companies that opened child-care centers in the 1980s realized how difficult it is to operate them. Other companies simply realize that they're not in the child-care business and prefer to have someone else run it for them. Child care was not considered one of their core competencies." The division, which has four sales reps, is being driven by a highly targeted marketing campaign. The division is zeroing in on three industries that have historically provided on-site child-care: health care, colleges and universities, and high technology. To reach decision makers in those industries, Kinder-Care is mounting a public relations campaign, conducting customized direct mailings to reach nearly one thousand companies or universities and advertising in the journals or magazines read by influentials in those industries. In addition, the company has exhibited at important trade shows in targeted industries or for human resources professionals.

Kinder-Care is now managing about twenty child-care centers for companies such as CIGNA Insurance, Citicorp, and Walt Disney World, where it opened a third center in 1992. Kinder-Care is also operating centers for such academic institutions as the University of Kentucky and Oregon State University. In addition, the company plans to take over or establish twenty-five more corporate child-care centers in 1993. "Employee-sponsored centers will be our greatest area of growth in the 1990s. It's also an area that will be highly competitive," according to Kaegi, who notes La Petite has opened about fifteen employer-sponsored centers.

Focusing on the Whole Child

Under the direction of Dr. Marcia Guddemi, Kinder-Care's vice president of education, the Montgomery, Alabama-based company has repackaged its instructional programs to recognize the social, physical, emotional, and intellectual development of a child. Kinder-Care sees to it that the four elements of a child's development are all properly nurtured. "Americans typically and naively put their trust in the wrong priority. They say I want my child to know his numbers, colors, and his ABCs before he goes to school because I want him to be competitive, and it's really not the right thing to do. The right thing to do is have an emotionally balanced child who can go to school and learn at a very rapid rate, because before they go to school they're going to learn at whatever rate they want to learn at. They need to be playing. They need to be experiencing the world and learning about

shapes by playing with shapes or learning about emotions by playing with other kids. Those are the kinds of things we're talking about
in whole child development. A child needs to be a child before he or
she can become a grown-up."

*I think you have to deliver on price, performance,
quality, and support, particularly in our business
where success is really measured by your repeat business. You don't make money on that first sale. The
profit is made on the repeat buyers."*

—GREG HERRICK, CHAIRMAN, PRESIDENT, AND CEO
OF ZEOS INTERNATIONAL

When Zeos International issued its first shares of stock in 1987, it
wooed investors with the promise of developing a computer circuit
board that was to be faster and more powerful than the standard
IBM PC motherboards.

But development of the touted Zeos motherboards soon hit a
snag, sending company founder Greg Herrick scrambling for alternatives to keep revenue flowing. "We had the public's money, and they
wanted to see some results." It was a twist of fate that would soon
change Herrick's life, and set the struggling Zeos on a course to
become the fastest-growing company in America.

"We decided to sell some PCs through mail order while we were
waiting for this board to be finished," says forty-one-year-old Herrick. "As it turned out, we never did sell the motherboards. We just
ended up selling PCs."

The first ad Herrick ran—a one-page black-and-white spot in
Computer Shopper—made little impact. "We adjusted some of the
features of the computer and the price, and the next ad did a little
better. After the third ad, the phones really started ringing." The
orders came in so fast, in fact, that Herrick's ear literally starting
bleeding from taking phone calls. "I couldn't even hold the phone
to my ear."

While the recent slump in the cutthroat personal computer market has taken some of the wind out of the company's sales, its rise to prominence was one of the great success stories in the computer industry. Zeos's revenues jumped from $1.7 million in 1987 to $230 million in 1991. *Fortune* magazine listed Zeos as the fastest-growing company in America, and *Investor's Daily* ranked it as the fastest-growing computer company. The St. Paul manufacturer managed to achieve hypergrowth through vigorous, relentless marketing and exhaustive attention to detail.

RAGS TO RICHES

Herrick's personal fortune is well into the millions now, but as he was building his business through the 1980s he had to wonder whether the eighty-hour weeks he was putting in would ever pay off.

He founded the company in 1981. His first product was a radio transmitter used by real estate agents to broadcast prerecorded sales messages for homes on the market that prospective home buyers could pick up on their car radios. Later the company began manufacturing computer circuit boards and other electronic components primarily as a subcontractor for other manufacturers.

Along the way, times were so hard and money so tight that Herrick had to sell his car and use the company delivery van for his basic transportation. "Try taking a girl out on a date in a delivery van. They aren't too excited about that." At one point, just to make the payroll, Herrick had to take out cash advances on his three Master-Cards and his three Visas.

Another time, with his company on the verge of collapse, Herrick resorted to even more desperate measures to collect an $18,000 debt from one of his customers. "They refused to pay the bill. Finally I said, 'We have about $350,000 of your inventory in our possession (because they would send the parts over to us to be assembled and we would deliver them back) and if I don't have your money by tonight, I'm going to throw it all in the Mississippi River.' He said, 'Well, I just can't get the money for you.' I said, 'Okay, I guess you're going to lose this inventory, because if you don't give me the money, we're going to be out of business anyway.'"

By three P.M. that day, the customer had relented, and Herrick had the check in hand. "And we continued doing business with them. It's lessons like that that really teach you the value of a dollar."

COMPETITIVE EDGE

Now that Zeos is well established in the computer business—with more than seven hundred employees and computer sales of thousands of units per month—the challenge for Herrick is sustaining the company's market share growth. He considers *value*—which he defines as "price, performance, quality, and support"—to be one of Zeos's key competitive advantages. Nothing particularly revolutionary there, admits Herrick, "but I think you have to deliver on those words, particularly in our business where success is really measured by your repeat business. You don't make money on that first sale. The profit is made on the repeat buyers.

"You can have the cheapest computer on the market, but if its performance is extremely slow, what good is it? On the other hand, you may have a computer that works 3 percent faster, but if you charge too high a price for it, people may not perceive that as value either. You have to strike a balance."

Zeos backs up its commitment to value in a number of ways.

TWENTY-FOUR-HOUR TOLL-FREE TECHNICAL SUPPORT LINE

Most computer companies run their technical support phone lines eight hours a day, five days a week. Most are standard phone lines—you make the call, you pay the toll. In fact, Microsoft has gone one step further—a 900 number for customers with technical questions—you call, you pay a hefty minute-by-minute service charge (even while you're on hold!). Not Zeos. The company offers a toll-free technical support line twenty-four hours a day, 365 days a year. "When people have problems with their computer, it's not always during normal working hours," says Herrick. "A lot of people work on their computers in the evenings or on weekends. We're here twenty-four hours a day—both sales and service."

COMPUTERS NOW

Under the company's standard delivery policy—which it dubs "Computers Now"—if you order your Zeos computer by one P.M., the order will be shipped out that day. "In fact," says Herrick, " if you want to pay the extra shipping rate, we can have the computer to you the very next day."

THE Z-CARD

The company has its own credit card, called the Z-Card (administered by Household Finance), that works just like a typical department store credit card. "We have thousands of Z-Card holders. It gives them one more line of credit they can tap into. For us, the Z-Card has a high close ratio and good reorder rate. If you're going to go to the trouble of filling out a form and making application, chances are you're interested in buying."

STAYING AHEAD OF THE MARKET.

"We try to get out of a product category six months before it dies." The intention is to create an image that Zeos is at the leading edge of the market. When Zeos introduced the 386 desktop, it stopped selling the 286 models altogether—even though they still made up 40 percent of the desktop market. The company's standard response to customers who requested the slower 286 models was, "Why would you want a 286 when we can sell you a 386SX for a 286 price?"

GEARING PRODUCT INTRODUCTIONS TO MAGAZINE SPECIALS

Herrick and his staff stay in constant contact with the editors of the leading computer magazines, they regularly attend conferences sponsored by the publishing companies, and they review editorial calendars for the coming year. "We know what the feature stories are going to be months in advance for all of the major computer magazines in the country, and we take that into account when we're doing our product planning. If they're talking about doing a review for a 586 computer, and Intel reps are talking to us about having a 586 chip ready, then it's pretty obvious to us that we should be considering having a 586 machine ready [in time for the magazine reviews]."

STRONG ADVERTISING

No one in the mail-order computer business spends more on advertising than Zeos. The company does about $2 million a month in advertising, placing most of its ads in computer periodicals such as *PC Magazine*. Zeos has also started advertising on the *Prodigy* computer on-line network and touts its notebook computers in in-flight magazines.

PUSHING THE PRODUCT

Zeos blankets the monthly computer magazines with ads—including as many as twenty to twenty-five pages of full-color ads in a single issue. For example, a recent issue of *PC Magazine* included these Zeos ads:

- A two-page ad on the Zeos 386-SX20.

- A two-page ad on the Zeos Notebook computer.

- A 13-page ad (including fold-out pages) on the full line of Zeos models.

- A one-page ink-jetted ad that addresses subscribers by name ("Hey John Smith, Check it out. Zeos has hot new upgradables . . . ").

- A one-page ad on its Z-Card and leasing program—also addressing subscribers by name—along with a double-page tear-out application form.

"We're the largest advertiser of computer hardware in computer trade publications. We're making sure the message continues to get out."

One of the biggest advertising coups for Zeos has been its personalized ink-jet ads in *PC Magazine.* "We get letters all the time from people saying, 'Boy, that's really neat. How did you get my name in there?' It creates a point of difference between ourselves and the other guys." In fact, Zeos negotiated an exclusive lock on all the ink-jetting for *PC Magazine* for a full year. "The magazine only had two stations that could do the ink-jetting, and we locked them up for a year. We were the only ones who could do it."

COPY HEAVY

Zeos ads tend to be very copy heavy, a policy Herrick contends has been vital to the company's success. "A lot of people say, 'Who in the world is going to read all of this?'" says Herrick. "Well, we don't really care if 95 percent of the people don't read it as long as the 5 percent who are about to make a purchase decision do. If you're about to spend a couple thousand dollars on a computer, you want all the information you can get—particularly if you're going to buy it sight unseen over the telephone."

The company's strategy is to give the price, show a large color picture of the computer, differentiate its models from the competition, and invite comparison to other computers. "The average computer buyer is going to call half a dozen companies so you want to lay out some points to look for—and basically give them enough information to be reasonably confident that this is a good company and that they are about to make a good purchase decision."

The final component of the company's strategy, contends Herrick, is persistence. "Persistence is the key to success in any business—persistence in taking your knocks and learning from it and going back and correcting it. You just keep trying."

We are convinced that advertising no longer sells products today. People do. I think a lot of people are wasting a lot of money on advertising, and I don't want to be one of them.

—HORST RECHELBACHER, FOUNDER AND CEO
OF AVEDA CORPORATION

Growing up in an impoverished section of Klagenfurt, Austria, Horst Rechelbacher had just one aspiration: to become a famous hairdresser. Salon apprentice at age fourteen in Klagenfurt, heralded stylist in Rome at seventeen, Rechelbacher's dream came true early in life.

Now, at fifty-one, Rechelbacher finds himself in a dream no schoolboy from Klagenfurt could ever have envisioned. He owns and directs Aveda Corporation, which, with revenues of more than $100 million a year, has become one of the fastest-growing personal care products companies in the world.

Rechelbacher first began to market his "all-natural" shampoos—made entirely from herbs, flower resins, and other natural ingredients—in the 1970s. It was a concept, recalls Rechelbacher, that was greeted with a lot of yawns—particularly from the independent hair care distributors he tried to persuade to sell his products.

"People looked at me like I was crazy," he says. "The salespeople didn't want to hear what I had to say." That was before the age of the ecologically enlightened consumer. Business is suddenly booming for Aveda, which has expanded its product line to some seven hundred different all-natural offerings—conditioners, perfumes, creams, lipsticks, hand soap, dish soap, cleansers, herbal teas, candles, and fragrances.

Rechelbacher already sells his Aveda products through nearly twenty-five thousand independent hair salons and a handful of his own "Esthetique" retail outlets. A fair start, says Rechelbacher, but he is gearing up for an explosion of growth he hopes will push Aveda's sales over $1 billion a year.

GETTING STARTED

It was never Horst Rechelbacher's intention to get into the manufacturing business. He was content to travel the world, styling the locks of the rich and famous, lecturing, teaching, and consulting for companies like Revlon and L'Oreal.

Only by accident—literally—did Rechelbacher gravitate to the retail end of the trade. During a stopover in Minneapolis, a drunken driver smashed into Rechelbacher's Jaguar, breaking his vertebrae and putting him in the hospital for several months. When Rechelbacher got out, he was prohibited from returning to Europe until his hospital bill was paid in full.

To raise the money, Rechelbacher opened a salon—and later a styling school—in Minneapolis under the "Horst" name. That was in 1965. A few years later, he whipped up his first line of natural shampoos in his kitchen sink at home. "My interest in making products evolved because no one else was making natural products. They were mimicking that they were doing it, but they weren't really doing it. Everything was derived from petrochemicals."

Artist, photographer, author, Rechelbacher speaks on environmental issues with an evangelical fervor. "It's becoming clearer and clearer how everything on the planet is interlinked—symbiotically, systemically," he states between sips of carrot juice. "It's when we get creative, or sometimes narcissistic, because we think we can make it cheaper or better—that's when we turn synthetic, and I think that's when we produce side effects like waste—also called pollution. So I think we have a lot of cleaning up to do. I call that the new 'eco (as in ecology) nomics.' It opens up a lot of possibilities for business."

ESTABLISHING THE ECOLOGICAL NICHE

With his round-rimmed spectacles and dark, flowing hair, Rechelbacher bears a slight resemblance to the late John Lennon. A *very* youthful fifty-one, he once lived briefly with the monks of the Himalayas and has traveled the back roads of the world, studying indigenous cultures and searching for herbs, flowers, and plants to use in his products. "I was looking for magical formulas," he says. He and his staff continue to tap the expertise of elders and medicine men in Nepal, Kenya, Malaysia, India, Australia, and South and North America to uncover new plants and natural ingredients for Aveda products.

Rechelbacher has put that same ecological spin on the day-to-day operation of his business. The company cafeteria serves nothing but organically produced foods. All company correspondence is printed on recycled paper. The company's 272,000 square-foot headquarters and manufacturing facility, located about ten miles north of Minneapolis, has a large employee exercise room, a handball court, and a basketball court for employees. A network of hiking and running trails crisscross the company's sixty-five-acre grounds. "We even have a full-time clinical psychologist who is like our medicine man," says Rechelbacher. "He takes care of the emotional part of the people."

Aveda has also donated hundreds of thousands of dollars to environmental causes and was the first corporation to sign the Valdez Principles, an international creed that seeks tough answers to global pollution.

SPREADING THE WORD

The first herbal shampoo Rechelbacher concocted was a rich brown concentrate. "I was so proud of it, but people who didn't have brown hair wouldn't use it," he recalls. So he developed four more shampoos—one each for red, blond, black, and silver hair.

Rechelbacher initially produced the shampoos strictly for his own salons in Minneapolis, but the products soon caught on with stylists from around the country who attended courses at his academy. "I never thought that I could become a big product manufacturer. It never dawned on me until people started asking for my shampoos."

In the late 1970s, Rechelbacher began to line up distributors for his products, and began to push them at conventions and seminars where he spoke. The early days were very rough. "I would try to convince these salespeople that they should sell Aveda products. Little did I realize that the game in the industry was, you better have deals, spiffs, give some TVs away, if you wanted people to sell your products. I walked in and all I had was herbs. I was telling people they should stop drinking, they should stop smoking, they should clean up their life and sell our herbal shampoos."

Response was far from overwhelming. But in every session, Rechelbacher reached a few people who embraced the concept and were willing to push Aveda products. Little by little, seminar after seminar, convention after convention, Rechelbacher began to generate a national demand for his shampoos.

DIRECT DISTRIBUTION

"I soon realized that you don't want to work with distributors who sell other people's products. You won't get the kind of commitment to your products that you need to make the line successful." To strengthen his sales effort, Rechelbacher began to establish his own network of distributors who sold only Aveda. Most of his distributors were hair care professionals who had attended his seminars and, as Rechelbacher puts it, "related to my paradigms." Many of them continued to work as hairdressers full time, selling Aveda in their spare hours.

At the same time he continued to hammer away at some of the big distributors. "I convinced them over the years that Aveda deserves focus. That gave us an experienced sales force that was focused on Aveda."

Rechelbacher has resolutely steered away from the spiffs and other incentives his competitors use to encourage salespeople to push their products. "We never gave anything away. I never felt that buying distributors or buying people to buy your products would work because it doesn't come from the heart."

LINE EXTENSION

As Aveda's hair care products became more in demand, Rechelbacher felt that the best way to grow the business would be to extend the line to other natural personal care products, such as perfumes and cosmetics, and home care products such as cleansers and detergents.

"Everybody in marketing and finance thought I was crazy for making all these products. They said, we are selling to hairdressers, how can we sell all these other products?"

Rechelbacher had the answer. He opened a concept store in Manhattan called Aveda Esthetique that carried all seven hundred of his environmental products. "It was the smartest thing I've ever done because that's the future of Aveda," he claims. He quickly opened several other Esthetiques—in Beverly Hills, Minneapolis, Vienna, and Washington, D.C.

"We'll have fifty stores in no time," says Rechelbacher. He anticipates opening as many as five hundred Esthetiques in the next five years. "We have an enormous waiting list of people who want to open the stores." Along with the store expansion, he also plans to continue to expand his product line. Aveda is developing a line of teas and other foods, and may also move into clothing.

MULTILEVEL SALES

To generate further interest in Aveda products, Rechelbacher has set up a multilevel marketing structure similar to Amway. "I'm running it like a political campaign. The flagship stores are the campaign headquarters. The people who own the flagship stores are responsible to go out into the community and educate the community." Salespeople can work their way up from one level to the next by meeting specific sales quotas:

Level One. New sales recruits begin by selling hair care products primarily to their personal network of acquaintances.

Level Two. Salespeople who meet hair care sales quotas can move up to color cosmetics and skin care product sales.

Level Three. The next step up is trainer, which authorizes the person to recruit other salespeople. The trainers get the word out primarily through group presentations. "We're never going to bang on doors. We're going to let Mary Kay and Avon do that. We want to educate corporations, we want to go into clubs, fraternities, organizations—we want to go where people meet. People always need speakers for their meetings."

Level Four. Success as a state or regional trainer will lead to appointment as a national trainer. "Then you are participating nationally in our campaign," says Rechelbacher. "You are training other professionals."

ADVERTISING AND PROMOTIONS

Traditional advertising media play a minor role in Aveda's overall marketing effort. The company spends only about $3 million a year in advertising.

"We are convinced that advertising no longer sells products today," says Rechelbacher. "People do. I think a lot of people are wasting a lot of money on advertising, and I don't want to be one of them." Instead, Aveda augments its direct-sales effort with a promotional campaign that uses several innovative alternatives to conventional advertising, including the following:

- A series of television infomercials.

- A broad promotional effort with buttons and T-shirts.

- Mail-order catalogs.

- Trade and consumer magazine display ads.

Rather than use the traditional approach—beautiful models posing with their lush lipstick or shimmering hair—a recent Aveda campaign featured Pinocchio with his long nose. The theme of the campaign was that claims by other manufacturers that they use "natural" ingredients in their personal care products are often misleading.

The major driving force in Aveda's marketing campaign, however, will continue to be the personal, direct contacts with customers through seminars, conventions, and multilevel relationships.

Rubbermaid has one of the fastest product development cycles in the world today. These two ads announce some of Rubbermaid's new products for ecologically minded consumers, one of the newest and fastest growing market segments. (*Courtesy Rubbermaid*)

Rough Tote® Recycling Container

Easy-access swing lid

Stackable in 3 sizes

Made from 20% post-consumer recycled plastic

No fuss is a recycling plus

Don't you wish everything was made like

Nasty. Sort.

Sort of reluctant to recycle? Sort it out with Rubbermaid's complete line of convenient recycling products. Many, like these, are made of at least 15% post-consumer recycled plastic. So doing the right thing just got easier.

Don't you wish everything was made like

Logitech knows that different computer users want different mice. In this ad it calls attention to its diverse product line. (*Courtesy Woolward & Partners, San Francisco*)

One Style Of Mouse For Everyone Makes About As Much Sense As One Style Of Shoe.

Shoemakers knew long before the term "workstation ergonomics" was invented: form should follow function and individual fit.

That's why we're offering seven ergonomic variations of the world's most useful input device.

All our mice are totally Microsoft® compatible and guaranteed to work with every Windows™ and DOS application.

And all are backed by the only company that developed and made over 15 million mice before making yours.

The most comfortable mouse for you is waiting at your Logitech dealer.

WE'D LIKE TO MATCH THEIR NEW FARES, BUT WE'D HAVE TO RAISE OURS.

No matter what the competition may come up with, Southwest Airlines' everyday low unrestricted fares are still lower than the Big Three. That's a fact that can save you a lot of money every day.

And unlike our competitors, with our low unrestricted fares, we don't charge you a penalty when your plans change. Which makes our fares the smart choice for you and your company. Always have been. Always will be.

SOUTHWEST AIRLINES
Just Plane Smart.
1-800-I-FLY-SWA
(1-800-435-9792)

Southwest Airlines emphasizes short haul, high frequency service with low fares. It is so successful because its low fares pull drivers out of their cars and onto its planes. (*Courtesy Southwest Airlines*)

Pitney Bowes, faced with a stagnant market and a stodgy image, revitalized itself by redesigning its postal machines to fit the new needs of businesses—and to easily take advantage of new postal rates. (*Courtesy Pitney Bowes*)

Stanhome's Enesco division produces quality collectible porcelain pieces. It responded to surging demand by *limiting* production, thereby increasing the long-term value of its products and their collectibility. (*Courtesy Stanhome*)

For a century OshKosh B'Gosh
made work clothes for farmers.
Facing a declining market, it moved
into children's clothing, drawing on
its time-honored American classics.
Ninety-six percent of its sales are
now to the children's market.
(*Courtesy Franklin, Laughlin &
Constable, Inc.*)

Sand Castles

Secrets

Dirty Hands

Missing Hamsters

Helping

Make Believe

Blankies

Bedtime Stories

Kids

OshKosh B'Gosh

OSHKOSH
B'GOSH
THE GENUINE ARTICLE

As genuine as ever.

Are you being told the truth about natural?

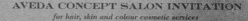

Aveda's all-natural products adhere to strict standards of purity, unlike some of its competitors', a fact which this ad draws attention to. (*Courtesy Aveda*)

McDonald's keeps its marketing fresh by appealing to every consumer group, taking care not to neglect anyone. These are three stills from its "Golden Time" ads. (*Courtesy McDonald's*)

PictureTel emphasizes the ease and comfort of using its videoconferencing equipment, which transmits images instantaneously, as opposed to traveling by plane for hours—an approach that is winning over customers at a flying clip. (*Courtesy PictureTel*)

Software Publishing included its "demo disk" (shown here) in a specially targeted ad in *PC Magazine*. The results exceeded the company's wildest expectations as PC users proved unable to resist their software after seeing just a little of what it could do. (*Courtesy Software Publishing*)

"We intend to produce and sell only those chemicals that can be manufactured, used and disposed of in a safe manner."

— from the Nalco Philosophy of Operation - 1984

The decade of the 90s has ushered in heightened concern for the environment. Nalco, through the development of environmentally responsible technology involving water treatment, air pollution control and waste minimization continues to play an active role in helping industry prevent and solve environmental problems.

NALCO CHEMICAL COMPANY
ONE NALCO CENTER ▯ NAPERVILLE, ILLINOIS 60563-1198

Photo courtesy of Nalco employee Cheryl Wisniewski

Nalco Chemical was suffering from the woes of rust-belt manufacturing, the main customer base for its water treatment services, when it redirected its technology and products to helping companies protect the environment, a field which is growing rapidly and sure to continue growing for years to come. (*Courtesy Nalco*)

TAXING QUESTION:

Can cities find sources of revenue other than taxes?

EDS helped Chicago answer a definite yes.

FAIR QUESTION:

Do businesses owned by minorities and women really have equal opportunity?

EDS could help you answer yes.

EDS takes over companies' information processing needs and not only saves them money through economies of scale but makes them money by applying its expertise to their businesses and increasing their productivity. (*Courtesy EDS*)

TOUGH QUESTION:

When your customers get more for their money, will they get it from you?

EDS helped Detroit Diesel answer yes.

TIMELY QUESTION:

When your customers need to buy again, will they buy from you?

EDS helped Kmart answer yes.

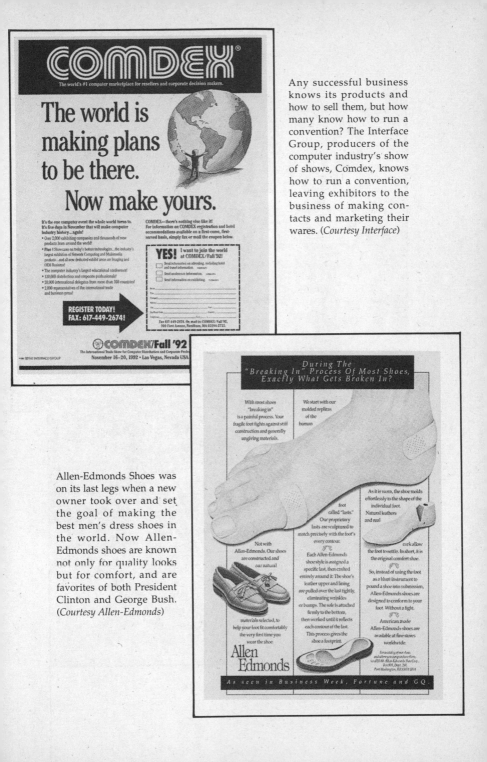

Any successful business knows its products and how to sell them, but how many know how to run a convention? The Interface Group, producers of the computer industry's show of shows, Comdex, knows how to run a convention, leaving exhibitors to the business of making contacts and marketing their wares. (*Courtesy Interface*)

Allen-Edmonds Shoes was on its last legs when a new owner took over and set the goal of making the best men's dress shoes in the world. Now Allen-Edmonds shoes are known not only for quality looks but for comfort, and are favorites of both President Clinton and George Bush. (*Courtesy Allen-Edmonds*)

Rolling Rock suffered from a down-at-the-heels image and declining sales. To revive the flagging sales of its natural brew made from mountain spring water, it redesigned its bottles to draw on nostalgia for an earlier America, and sales doubled. (*Courtesy Rolling Rock*)

Link Technologies is a leading manufacturer of computer terminals because it can produce almost any terminal called for and make it a pleasure to use, as this ad emphasizes. (*Courtesy Link Technologies*)

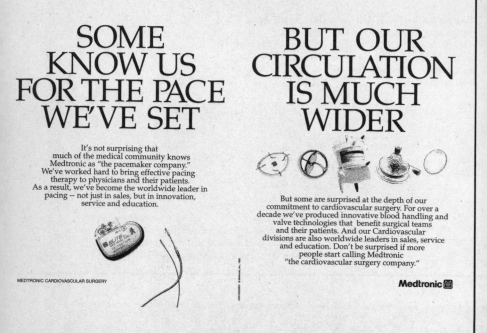
Medtronic succeeds in international markets by taking the battle to its competitors' home bases, where its technological lead makes it a tough adversary. (*Courtesy Medtronic*)

Brock Control Systems is a leading software designer, specializing in computer automating systems for sales and marketing that allow companies to devote creativity to selling and not to managing departments. Its greatest growth is now coming from Western Europe. (*Courtesy Brock Control Systems*)

YOU COULD KEEP SELLING THE SAME OLD WAY. BUT FOR HOW LONG?

The moral of the story is clear: you've got to change with the times or get left behind. Today, that means automating your sales and marketing. But which system is right for your company? And what kind of results can you expect?

At Brock Control Systems, we can answer all your questions about sales and marketing automation. We're the leading provider of complete marketing and sales productivity systems. And the only company that can automate your entire business cycle.

Brock's Activity Manager Series™ is designed with an open architecture that's readily integrated into existing environments. It arrives ready to start increasing productivity from day one. Yet you can easily customize it to match your needs exactly. Or let our professionals do it for you.

Companies that have already automated their sales and marketing are gaining more than an edge. They're gaining momentum. So don't wait to find out what Brock can do for you. Call now for more information.

1-800-221-0775

 BROCK CONTROL SYSTEMS, INC.

The future of sales.™

© 1990 Brock Control Systems, Inc.

Reader Service #111

Sybaritic's Alphamassage® health capsule is becoming a favorite of Hollywood actors and European jet-setters in addition to well-heeled health-conscious middle Americans. (*Courtesy Sybaritic*)

Customers are looking for four things when they come into the store: They want a terrific product, they want fabulous service, they want a clean store, and they want a good deal. You do those four things, and people are going to come back.

—FRED DELUCA, PRESIDENT OF
SUBWAY SANDWICHES

In 1982, with a grand total of two hundred restaurants in his Subway sandwich system, founder Fred DeLuca announced his goal for the following twelve years at a company meeting. "I said I wanted to have five thousand stores by 1994," recalls DeLuca. "Everyone looked at me like I was nuts."

But DeLuca's grandiose objectives would in fact prove conservative. The company hit the goal well ahead of schedule and was up to seven thousand Subway franchises by the end of 1992. The privately held firm posts about $1.5 billion a year in sales.

The real breakthrough for DeLuca came when he turned to franchising. Instead of trying to open and operate every shop himself, he began selling the concept to entrepreneurs in search of an opportunity. Over the past five years, Subway has become the fastest-growing franchise operation in the world—ever. It opens, on average, about three new stores a day: one thousand stores a year. But with three thousand other franchise-based companies out there—including more than four hundred franchise restaurant groups—the pressure is always on to attract new, qualified entrepreneurs to keep the growth booming.

ATTRACTING FRANCHISEES

In 1965, at age seventeen and looking for a way to finance his college education, DeLuca opened his first submarine sandwich shop in Bridgeport, Connecticut. He used $1,000 in seed money from a family acquaintance, Dr. Peter Buck, who has remained a silent partner. Business was so slow the first six months that DeLuca nearly gave it up. But after conferring with Buck, DeLuca decided instead to open more stores, to increase the restaurant's visibility. By the end of the first full year, he had opened a total of four shops in Bridgeport—and

Subway was off and running. By 1978, Subway boasted one hundred shops—thirteen years after the first one opened.

More than half of the thousand new Subway shops each year are opened by existing franchise operators. The balance are opened by new owners who either hear about Subway through word of mouth, or see an ad for franchise opportunities in newspapers or magazines.

DeLuca points to a handful of factors that have aided his success in attracting new owners: low initial investment, high long-term potential, on-going support, and high visibility.

RIGHT PRICE

"We know we're competing with a lot of other franchise opportunities out there," says DeLuca. "So we've tried to price this in such a way that it makes sense for new owners."

Costs include:

- Franchise fee, $10,000.

- Equipment, $25,000 to $30,000.

- Remodeling, $25,000.

- Inventory, rent security deposit, and other costs: $5,000 to $15,000.

"The average store, completely built and paid for, costs around $75,000," says DeLuca. "But we also try to make it easier for new owners by helping them finance or lease the equipment package from Subway ($2,500 down and a five-year-payment plan). That knocks the initial cost of opening a franchise down to about $50,000."

Most franchise owners also seek financial assistance from banks or other lenders. Once a Subway shop is up and running, it can generate up to $800,000 a year in total revenue.

In contrast, new McDonald's franchise owners face about $1.3 million in up-front expenses, although they can finance the bulk of that through McDonald's.

"McDonald's provides a lot of the financing for its franchise owners," says DeLuca. "When you think about a big operation like that, I don't know if it's really good to have somebody who can write a check for a million bucks. Is he really going to work for the store?" McDonald's prefers roll-up-the-sleeves-type owners who will manage the stores to build up business. DeLuca prefers the same and offers new owners a great deal of assistance to help them succeed.

PREPARING FOR SUCCESS

Each new franchise owner is required to take a two-week training course at the Subway headquarters in Connecticut that includes everything from making the sandwiches to balancing the books. "We rely a lot on training people to be successful in the proper way," says DeLuca. "We can teach somebody to make a sandwich in five minutes, but what we really focus on is how to make money in this business."

Trainees spend about half the time in the store and half the time in the classroom. The training includes:

- Assembly of sandwiches.

- General store operation.

- Cost control modules to control food and labor costs.

- Cash control.

- Lectures on store design, store construction, and site location.

- Employee and customer relations.

The sessions focus strongly on cost controls. Owners are urged to measure their results on a frequent basis—and to calculate their labor costs and food costs to the point at which they know exactly the percentage of their weekly expenditures that goes to pay for olives, pickles, onions, and each of the other Subway ingredients. "That way they can see where there's deviation, and make the necessary corrections."

The training sessions tend to leave a strong impression on the new franchise owners. "It could never prepare you for everything that you're going to go through," says Tim Johnson, who now owns six Subway franchises in the Minneapolis area, "but the training really prepares you well for the paperwork and cost controls."

Adds DeLuca, "What we tell the owners is that the customers are looking for four things when they come into your store. They want a terrific product, they want fabulous service, they want a clean store, and they want a good deal. You do those four things, and people are going to come back. You can always bring people into the store, but it's more important that you bring them back. That's really where your business is."

FIELD SUPPORT

Subway has developed a strong field support system with a national network of 120 field officers, or "development agents," who help franchisees with site selection, advertising and promotional decisions, and other business operations. "They help you through the whole construction process, including design and site selection," says Johnson. "And then when you open your store, they work forty hours the first week to help get you started." The company also provides its franchisees with the following:

- *A weekly package from headquarters.* This includes a variety of news and information and an eight-page weekly newsletter with company updates, marketing suggestions, and new products.

- *Designees at headquarters.* The company has eighty designees, or coordinators, who handle about eighty stores apiece. "Every franchisee has his own specific coordinator he can call for assistance with headquarters-type work," says DeLuca. "That way, when you call in, you're not talking to just anybody, you have your special person you've developed a relationship with, so you know you can call in and get things done more easily."

SITE SELECTION

Selecting a site for new Subway stores is a joint process involving the franchisee and the regional Subway development agent—although the agent has final approval authority. DeLuca says the company looks for three key attributes at every site—people, visibility, and accessibility, the PVA strategy:

- *People.* "First of all you need people. You need traffic."

- *Visibility.* "Once you have the people, they have to be able to find your store. You want one of two types of visibility—either you want right-on-the-street visibility where the store stands out to all the passing traffic, or if it's in a shopping center, you want to be in a busy center where people can readily find you."

- *Accessibility*. "Once the people are there, how do they get from their car into your store." Each site is evaluated for parking availability and ease of access.

ADVERTISING

All franchisees are required to give 2 ½ percent of their total revenue to an advertising fund. About 35 percent of the money is used for national advertising and 65 percent is returned to the regions to be used for local advertising. Some local franchise groups also throw in an additional 1 to 2 percent to bolster advertising still further. Most of the company's advertising money goes to television spots, although the company also does radio, free-standing inserts in newspapers, and coupons through direct mail.

To coordinate national advertising and marketing decisions, the franchisees elect a national board of directors made up of eleven franchise owners. The board ensures that the franchisees are well represented in the marketing decision making.

CONTINUING THE GROWTH

With seven thousand Subway stores currently in operation, there already seems to be a shop in every well-placed shopping center and strip mall in America. Can the growth possibly continue at the present torrid rate? DeLuca believes it can, although the company has already drawn criticism for expanding too rapidly. A 1992 article in *The Wall Street Journal* quoted several disgruntled former franchise owners who charged that the company's site selection process often leaves much to be desired, and that the company is "selling too many franchises too close together." The problem has been a financial nightmare for more than a few owners. The *Journal* quoted Subway documents that showed that 40 percent of the twenty-three hundred Subway shops listed as open or preparing to open at the end of 1987 either changed hands, relocated, closed down, or never opened.

Even at that, however, Subway's success rate far exceeds the national average for new businesses. About 80 percent of all nonfranchised new businesses fold within the first three years.

DeLuca points out that the alternative to too many stores is too few stores and very little visibility. "To me," adds Johnson, "there's a Subway just about everywhere there should be. People aren't going to travel that far to go to Subway. So it's better to have a Subway in every key part of town—everywhere you need one." In fact, even with its seven thousand shops, Subway still trails McDonald's, which has about three thousand more restaurants than Subway in the U.S. market. "I think we can support at least as many stores as McDonald's," claims DeLuca.

Subway is also following McDonald's lead into the international market. The company recently opened a store in Tokyo, which set the all-time single store sales volume record its very first week. McDonald's has about three thousand restaurants outside the United States, and DeLuca would like to see Subway follow suit. "McDonald's is blazing the trail for us in the international market."

I think experimentation is always important. Innovation comes from a lot of experimentation. . . . But the customer always comes back to tell us what they're comfortable with, and what they feel is the McDonald's image. They cast their vote at the cash register.

—DAVID GREEN, SENIOR VICE PRESIDENT OF MARKETING
FOR MCDONALD'S CORPORATION

When your target audience is everyone who eats, achieving market penetration is no small potatoes. That's one of the many challenges facing McDonald's as it tries to keep its unblemished string of more than twenty-five consecutive years of record profits intact. While the Oak Brook, Illinois, operation remains far and away the world's leading fast-food restaurant chain, the challenge of keeping customers filing through the golden arches has never been more demanding.

"The quick-service restaurant business is one of the most competitive businesses you can be in right now," concedes David Green, McDonald's senior vice president of marketing. But McDonald's still has a leg up on the rest of the fast-food business. "The thing that continues to differentiate McDonald's from the rest of the industry is the persona we've developed over the past thirty-five years. More than almost any other brand in the world, we have established a personality, an image, an enduring reputation with our customers. You could even say we've become a cultural icon."

Maintaining that status as cultural icon—and profitable business—requires a Herculean marketing effort on many fronts.

REACHING THE MASSES

With its multiple target groups, McDonald's must simultaneously pursue several very different advertising campaigns. "You have to talk to each demographic group individually," says Green, "and you have to say to them, essentially, 'We understand you, we understand your lifestyle, we understand your culture, and you're important to us.' But we still have to approach them all from the same personality.

"I've seen other companies who tried to talk to one target group in a way that would be diametrically opposed to their approach with a different target group," adds Green. "That's not what McDonald's stands for. We have a consistent personality, and then we customize our approach within that personality to reach each demographic segment."

The primary target markets for McDonald's include the following.

KIDS AND FAMILIES

This was the first group McDonald's targeted—with Ronald McDonald leading the way—and it continues to be the company's primary focus with its Happy Meals and special promotions.

"Our emphasis on children has always been a key to our success."

TWEENS

Tweens are those who are "too old for Ronald but too young for the car keys." A notoriously tough audience, tweens don't want to be talked down to. They do want to be spoken to candidly, and they want to feel that you understand them. "We prepare specific commercials for this group with a cast of characters doing the kinds of things that that age group really enjoys doing. We try to make every ad relevant to the audience we're targeting."

YOUNG ADULTS

Young adults are between the ages of eighteen and thirty-four. "These are people who are starting their careers, starting their families. Our message is that we are available to them, that we understand their life-style, their time needs, their need to get a meal quickly and efficiently," explains Green.

MINORITIES

McDonald's was the first major retailer to hire an agency specifically for black and for Hispanic consumer marketing. The company runs a number of commercials geared specifically to both groups, including Spanish-language ads on the Hispanic cable networks. The McDonald's personality is still present in all the commercials, but each commercial emphasizes something relevant to Hispanic or African-American culture. "Something is going to happen in that spot where they can say, 'Hey, McDonald's understands.' That's what breeds brand loyalty." McDonald's reaches out for its customers.

SENIORS

In its target marketing for the seniors, McDonald's pushes the economic aspect of its meals. It also encourages seniors to apply for employment positions at its restaurants.

STAYING THE COURSE

The McDonald's persona of a clean, wholesome, economical family restaurant has remained consistent for nearly four decades, since the late Ray Kroc bought the first restaurants. "We represent basic family values. Whether you see it in our advertising, how we treat people in our stores, the decor, the innovations we've added, it all stems from these basic values we've had for thirty-five years."

And should the company stray off course, the customers always steers it back. "The customer understands who we are sometimes even better than we do." A "Hot Dog McNuggets" that was tested regionally several years ago fizzled badly, as did a "Hoola Burger" created by Ray Kroc. "It was a toasted piece of pineapple on a bun," recalls Green. "It didn't even have a burger in it. And it didn't go over very well. The customer said, 'Wait a minute, I'm not sure that's who you are.'"

Despite the occasional failures, however, McDonald's will continue to test new waters. "I think experimentation is always important. Innovation comes from a lot of experimentation. We take a lot of risks by pushing the envelope as to what McDonald's is, but the customer always comes back to tell us what they're comfortable with, and what they feel is the McDonald's image. They cast their vote at the cash register."

THE LOCAL EMPHASIS

While major marketing and promotional campaigns emanate from the corporate office, pinpoint local marketing is often left up to the franchisees. "Part of the responsibility of each of our restaurant managers is to customize and target their message to the people who live in their trading areas."

In addition to the traditional advertising modes such as local radio and newspaper ads, McDonald's has the luxury of one other major medium—its own stores. "We have twenty-two million people a day coming through our restaurants. We reach more people and touch more people than some of the networks do."

To get the most mileage out of that daily exposure, McDonald's uses several on-site marketing tools, including:

• Tray liners highlighting certain products or promotions.

• Point-of-purchase displays and menu board displays.

• Calendars of coming special events.

The company's local franchisees are also encouraged to become involved in the community. They sponsor special programs, contribute to select causes, and in some cases, even open their restaurants for special seminars or workshops for nonprofit organizations. While it's hard to measure the bottom-line effect of their local involvement, there's no question that it earns the company a certain amount of goodwill from the community.

TAPPING THE ENTREPRENEURIAL SPIRIT

McDonald's counts on its franchisees not only to market its foods and spread goodwill in the local communities but also to provide suggestions for generating customer interest on a national level. "Each of our owner-operators brings entrepreneurial ideas and his or her own excitement to the business. They've given us some of our best ideas."

For instance, the Ronald McDonald House was started by a franchise owner in Philadelphia. The Happy Meals program was started by a marketing manager in St. Louis. The idea for special Halloween shakes came from another franchise owner, as did the suggestion to use *Indiana Jones* videos as part of a recent promotion.

The fountain of ideas coming from the owner-operator community and the employees keeps McDonald's fresh. "One of my jobs in marketing is to be the clearing center for these great ideas. As we see them grow in one part of the country, we pass the ideas on to other franchise owners elsewhere."

WHERE'S THE BEEF?

Amid all the special promotions, the Happy Meals, the on-site playgrounds, and the community involvement, the one element that nearly gets lost in the shuffle is the company's very reason for being: the food. The meal itself seems almost secondary to the total McDonald's experience—a fact that seems to be just fine with McDonald's marketers. Sell the sizzle—not the steak. "The food is very important, but there's more to McDonald's than the food. It's the experience and the feeling that you get when you go to McDonald's. That's a very important part of our success."

It's that experience that continues to give McDonald's an edge in the burger wars—particularly with children. "As one of our customers recently put it, the McDonald's store is one of the last bastions of true democracy. What he meant by that was, everyone is equal. It doesn't matter whether you're a child, a teenager, or an adult; whether you're black or Hispanic; whether you're old or young, you're all treated and respected in relatively the same manner at McDonald's. There are no barriers whatsoever. And I think a kid senses that.

"When you take a child to a white tablecloth restaurant, there's a different kind of feeling that he gets," says Green. "He has to act a little differently. At McDonald's, children get a sense that they can act like themselves. They're not going to be penalized for acting like children."

BUSINESS TO BUSINESS:
THE TOUGHEST SELL

MOST U.S. MARKETERS will never sponsor a thirty-second television spot during the Super Bowl, circulate dollar-off coupons, or erect point-of-purchase displays at a local retailer. That's not how to reach the buyers or buying committees of business products that range from mainframes to blast furnaces.

PictureTel knows how it's done. It invites prospective corporate buyers of its $20,000 video conferencing systems to half-day seminars around the country for a firsthand look. In some cases, prospects can bring one back to their own office for a trial run, a tactic designed to make it even tougher to resist signing on the dotted line.

Software Publishing Corporation (SPC) put the latest version of its popular business graphics software in the hands of thirty thousand hot prospects based on a demographic breakdown from the publisher of *PC Week* magazine. The publication then poly-bagged a free diskette that provided a self-guided demonstration of *Harvard Graphics for Windows*.

Sullivan Dental Products makes life less painful for America's dentists by getting them what they need in a hurry thanks to an alphanumeric coding system in the company catalog. Sullivan's toll-free order and customer service lines are all manned by former dental assistants—people with a special insight into their customers' business.

Octel Communications, marketer of voice mail systems, faces a marketing challenge similar to PictureTel: convincing corporate audiences that its technology can boost a company's productivity. Octel makes that point through nearly forty customer seminars a year along with videotaped testimonials of satisfied customers that are mailed to the CEOs of *Fortune* 500 companies.

Unique products require unique marketing strategies.

We are bringing the work to the people instead of bringing the people to work. In that context we are dramatically changing the culture of the way we do business.

—ROBERT F. MITRO, VICE PRESIDENT OF SALES AND
MARKETING AT PICTURETEL CORPORATION

The telephone of the future is about to ring. For forty years, futurists have been heralding the advent of the "picture phone," a telephone that would let you talk face-to-face with your callers. And for forty years, the technology—the ability to send video signals over telephone wires—has eluded researchers.

Scientists finally began to perfect the technology in the 1980s by breaking visual images into digitized signals that could be transmitted bit by bit. The only problem was price. A single picture phone unit—with receiver, monitor, camera, speakers, decoder, and control pad—ran into the hundreds of thousands of dollars.

All that is changing. By bringing down the cost of picture phone technology, PictureTel, the world's leading manufacturer of video conference systems, expects to put picture phones and video communications desktop computer software into millions of homes and businesses.

"We'll start shipping in the millions in the middle part of this decade," predicts Rob Mitro, PictureTel vice president of sales and marketing. As Mitro speaks, he gestures, he smiles, he leans forward in his chair. He is in Massachusetts; I am in Minnesota. It's my first encounter with the phone of the future. And, yes, it's everything the futurists predicted. Big screen, full color. You talk to the television; it talks back.

EXPLOSIVE GROWTH

You won't find many companies that could match the growth of PictureTel. Its revenue jumped from $4 million in 1988 to about $150 million in 1992—and all from selling a product that is dropping in price every bit as fast as the company's revenues are rising.

In the mid-1980s, the cost of a single video-conference system ran into the hundreds of thousands of dollars. By 1991, the price had dropped to just $20,000 for PictureTel's least expensive unit.

The drop in telephone line charges has been even more dramatic. In the mid-1980s, the long distance line charge was about $1,000 per hour because of the dedicated lines needed to handle the signals. Now, with advances in signal transmission capabilities, the per hour calling charge has dropped to just $12 to $25 an hour (roughly double the rate of a typical long distance call).

While line charges may not drop much further, unit costs are expected to continue to fall as the technology improves. The drop in unit costs has already stimulated an explosion in unit sales. PictureTel's estimated 1992 sales of about five to seven thousand units is nearly ten times the 1990 sales volume.

BRUTE FORCE MARKETING

Before coming to PictureTel, Rob Mitro spent seventeen years moving through the ranks of IBM. He arrived at PictureTel in 1988 as vice president of sales and marketing. What he found was a company with a great product but no clue as to how to get it to market.

"It was like going back to high school," recalls Mitro. "The founders of this company were two MIT students and their professor. They were still in their mid-twenties, and they had recruited a lot of people of the same age." The company was in desperate need of some senior management experience.

Mitro also saw a couple of other deficiencies:

- *No clear objectives.* "We needed a planning process to establish some goals, strategies and objectives for ourselves that were measurable and aggressive."

- *No marketing focus.* "I characterized the organization as being a mile wide and a micron deep. There was no marketing focus. We just threw whatever resources we had at whatever opportunities came along. I call it 'brute force marketing.' That's not atypical of entrepreneurial startup companies where they don't know where the next dollar is coming from. What happens is, the next guy through the door who says 'I'll buy something if you do the following things' is the one everyone focuses on. It's an 'opportunity du jour' kind of environment."

Mitro quickly narrowed the focus. "Rather than dissipate our energies by trying to do too many things and not doing anything well, we wanted to do fewer things and do them well—even at the expense of throwing some sacred cows over the side."

CORNERING THE MARKET

It is PictureTel's technology that has given it the edge in the marketplace worldwide. The company can put its systems on the market for less because it designs and produces its own high-performance microchips. PictureTel's low-end unit, (recently at $20,000), was selling at about 50 percent the cost of the nearest competitor, and its higher-end systems ran about 10 percent lower. Even at that, PictureTel's margins were consistently better because of its savings in production costs.

PictureTel has been trying use its position of strength to capture a dominant share of the market. "We need to be able to capture all the major channels of distribution," says Mitro. His marketing structure includes the following:

- PictureTel's own nationwide sales staff hired and trained to deal directly with *Fortune* 500 companies. "We made a major investment in building our own sales offices."

- Its own in-house nationwide service organization. "Initially we were going to contract with a third-party service organization, but, coming from an IBM background, I felt that customer satisfaction really begins with the order, the installation, and the maintenance.

It is important to maintain the relationship with the account by not only having a sales organization but also a service organization that is readily available."

Maintaining its own service organization has given PictureTel some competitive advantages. For example, PictureTel is the only vendor in America that will commit to next-day, on-site repair, if they cannot make the repair over the phone. In fact, the company even offers *same*-day repair guarantees to some larger customers.

• They have sales dealers for smaller companies. PictureTel has complemented its direct sales force with a network of telecommunications distributors, or dealers, it contracts with to focus on smaller 500 companies. "A crucial piece of our distribution strategy has been to avoid channel conflict. We want coverage without conflict. In this case, if the direct sales force gets a lead on a sub-*Fortune* 500 company, they give it to the dealers; if the dealers get a lead on a *Fortune* 500 company, they are obligated to give it to our direct sales force."

• PictureTel has established subsidiaries or trading partners in all major foreign markets.

STRATEGIC ALLIANCES

A major source of sales leads for PictureTel has come through its "strategic partnership" program. The company has established partnerships with many of the world's major communications carriers and switch manufacturers, including, among others, AT&T, Ameritech, MCI, Northern Telecom, Siemens, and Mitsubishi.

"Typically, one of our strategic partners like AT&T will bring us leads, and we pay them a co-marketing commission for that lead. If we are successful with that lead, we would get the equipment sale, and AT&T would get the digital switch network sale." It's a relationship that benefits both parties. "AT&T would probably tell you that 75 to 90 percent of its digital switch service sales are attributable to PictureTel. And we've made our product available through the thousand-person AT&T sales staff—which is a lot more coverage than we would ever get ourselves."

OTHER MEDIA

In addition to its sales force and strategic partner referrals, PictureTel uses several other media to get the word out about its products:

- *Print advertising.* PictureTel had never used media advertising until 1991 when the company began a series of ads in *The Wall Street Journal.* The ads, which focused on the falling price of PictureTel's video teleconference systems, drew a strong response from corporations who were not aware of how inexpensive the picture phone technology had become. "Most people who had looked into video conference systems in the past still thought it would cost them ten times what we are charging," says Mitro.

- *Trade shows.* Conventions and trade shows have long been a primary medium of exposure for the company. PictureTel is represented at nearly every major electronics show both in the United States and abroad.

- *Direct mail.* The company uses direct-mail marketing to target small- and mid-size companies.

But there is nothing that really sells the systems quite the way PictureTel seminars do.

THE PITCH

Periodically in every major city, PictureTel sponsors a series of half-day seminars to demonstrate its systems to prospects. The seminars tend to be very convincing.

Each seminar begins with a demonstration of the system and includes some information on PictureTel's full line of products and services. Then the PictureTel representative uses the system to call some of PictureTel's customers. "The first customer says, 'Here's how I justified the purchase of the system to the accountants.' The second customer says, 'Here's why I chose PictureTel.' The third customer is typically an international customer, and they can talk about that. So we're using the technology—and our customers—to sell the systems. It's a very powerful marketing program."

Persuading busy executives to take a few minutes of their time to explain why they bought the PictureTel system has been no problem.

"Once they've used the system, they become evangelists. They are on the leading edge of a brand new technology, and they are very excited and very proud to talk about how they have adapted this technology to grow their companies. We have no problem whatsoever in getting them to tell their story."

The major selling point customers drive home in their testimonials is the travel and time savings the systems facilitate. "You are saving more than just travel costs," says Mitro. "The real value is in the productivity savings of you not having to come here to meet me, or me not having to travel there to meet you. You are eliminating the dead time, the unproductive time when you are in an airplane, or even in a forty-five-minute cab ride across the city."

The other message is that PictureTel is bringing the work to the people instead of bringing the people to work. In that context video phones are dramatically changing the way the world does business.

Mitro cites the case of a company with manufacturing operations overseas. "They can talk about the style and colors they want, the manufacturer can show some samples or preliminary prototypes, and they can make a decision on what they want on the spot, and nobody had to travel anywhere. In terms of time-to-market, it can save a company weeks."

ONE ON ONE

Private demonstrations can sometimes work even better than the seminars. James Bell, a former regional director for PictureTel who now serves as an independent distributor for the company's products, says he often brings a customer in for a thirty-minute demonstration or, in some cases, loans out a demo system to give a company a chance to use it for a few days. "It's the puppy dog approach," Bell quips. "Let them take it home, and get used to using it, then see if they can bear to bring it back."

One rather unusual demonstration produced a very dramatic reaction. The chairman of a major U.S. manufacturer asked if he could conduct a video conference with the heads of his operations in Europe and Asia.

All the major players gathered in Atlanta, Belgium, and Hong Kong for a three-way conference. "I gave them a fifteen-minute overview of the equipment, set them up, and then I left," recalls Bell.

The executives conducted a five-hour marketing strategy meeting. After it was over, Bell met with the chairman and started to point out the travel cost savings of getting all the parties together by video conference.

"That's irrelevant," snapped the chairman. "I just conducted a meeting I couldn't have conducted otherwise without this technology. It takes four or five business days in travel time to get our international people in here for a day-and-a-half staff meeting, and they just don't have the time to do that each month. This is a strategic business tool we can't live without."

Sale closed.

THE INTERNATIONAL NETWORK

PictureTel has established a network of subsidiaries and sales partnerships in all the key markets around the world. One of the biggest problems the company faced in its global sales was determining how to divide up the revenues on multinational orders. In other words, a company in Germany might order systems for its offices in France and Japan. While the sale originates in Germany, the order, installation, and service of those units would have to come from PictureTel's distributors in France and Japan. The dilemma PictureTel has faced is, how do you fairly compensate all the participating offices? The company set up its "global multinational account partners program" that designates preordained revenue splits on all business that crosses national borders. "There are three pieces to it: the ordering piece, the selling piece, and the installing piece," explains Mitro. "On any given order, the same sales office might get all three-thirds of the pie (if it was sold, ordered, and installed within that country), or they might get two-thirds of the pie, or they might just get one-third." This compensation arrangement eliminates turf disputes and ensures uniform pricing for PictureTel systems around the world.

COMPUTERS: THE NEXT BIG WAVE

PictureTel recently established a strategic alliance with IBM to develop products for a video work station. By adding functions to IBM desktops, users will be able to convert their computers to PictureTel video stations and call up images from computer users around the world.

While costs at this stage of the program development would be prohibitive for most computer users, in full production PictureTel should be able to drive the cost down to a very affordable level.

By 1993, the company expects to be able to market the software and video add-ons for around $5,000. Ultimately, it should drop as low as $1,000 to $3,000. PictureTel anticipates the sale of millions of units by the middle of this decade. "We'll start turning them out like popcorn," he says. "It will become a fundamental, like the phone. First it will become ubiquitous in the business world, and then it will very quickly catch on in the consumer world."

We've succeeded by acing the marketing mix: product, price, promotion, packaging, and distribution. If you hit all those elements dead-on, if you know them cold, then success is less magic and good luck than it is good hard work.

—FRED M. GIBBONS, PRESIDENT AND CEO
OF SOFTWARE PUBLISHING CORPORATION

Software Publishing Corporation (SPC) customers who query the company's technical support or customer-service lines usually won't get away without answering a few questions about themselves.

Interrogation it's not. All SPC, the $143 million Santa Clara, California–based graphics software maker, really wants to know is such things as their names, companies, degrees of purchasing authority, and other software products they're interested in. But those simple answers are worth their weight in gold to SPC, which loads the responses into its ever-expanding customer database to better target its message to existing and prospective customers.

That database has become SPC's most powerful marketing tool. The company's flagship product, *Harvard Graphics for Windows*, allows users to create colorful charts, graphs, and illustrations to enhance business presentations and carries a list price of $595. "We get two thousand calls a week, a half million calls a year. It's an enormous opportunity for us to capture information about our customers as well as learn what they want from us," says Fred M. Gibbons, president and CEO.

MARKETING WITH NEW TECHNOLOGY

"It's very gratifying to put an advertising message out to millions of people. But it's also gratifying to use new technologies like customer data bases to get a high hit rate." After the customer information is loaded into the database, SPC conducts a search on that customer's particular interest and then puts together a classic "call to action" brochure, which it mails to the customer. Then, in many cases, the telemarketing group follows up with a personal call. This highly targeted approach integrates a customer database with product literature and telemarketing and converts 20 percent of the callers to SPC help lines into buyers of new or upgraded SPC products. Direct marketing experts say a 1 to 2 percent conversion rate is normal.

"It's a very good batting average. But remember, this is not a cold call. These are qualified people who either are our current customers or prospective customers who've taken the time to get in touch with us. We might be able to push that hit rate as high as 50 to 60 percent some day by continuing to ask those customers what they want next and then fine-tune those products to meet their tastes."

LAUNCHING FROM A DATABASE

SPC tapped a database to help launch *Harvard Graphics for Windows*. The company had to try a different tack to launch the product because, as Gibbons admits, SPC was three to six months behind the competition in introducing a business graphics program based on Microsoft Corporation's wildly popular *Windows* interface. Numerous software publishers are rapidly releasing more database, spreadsheet, and other applications for *Windows*.

Gibbons describes SPC's three biggest competitors as "Microsoft, the three hundred-pound gorilla; Lotus Development, the two hundred-pound gorilla; and Borland International, the one hundred-pound gorilla." He sees the competitive environment as "ruthless and bloody."

Although all of those diversified software makers are larger, SPC remains the market leader in the business graphics niche due to some rapid and creative adjustments. "We made a commitment to the *OS/2* operating system by IBM and we bet on the wrong horse. *Windows* was the horse to ride and we were on the wrong horse. We were going to be between three and six months behind our leading competitors. We needed a way to catch up. So we designed a marketing plan that would give us the maximum impact and get customers to look at us quickly. Every day counted."

Joining Forces

SPC enlisted *PC Week* magazine as a marketing partner in its plan to get corporate buyers of business presentation software to delay their purchasing plans until SPC trotted out its *Harvard Graphics for Windows* product. Key steps in the plan included the following:

- Identifying the names of thirty thousand *PC Week* readers who had purchasing authority for business presentations software.

- Sending a self-guided demonstration disk of the new product to those selected readers by hand-stuffing the poly-bagged disk and accompanying ad into the magazine.

- Calling the recipients of the demo disks and attempting to convert them into purchasers.

- Following up with a postlaunch series of ads in *PC Week* that featured a call to action.

The campaign's success was reflected on the company's record-setting second quarter results. *Harvard Graphics for Windows* was responsible for 40 percent of the company's revenues.

Pinpoint Accuracy

"Publications like *PC Week* have gotten increasingly sophisticated in their ability to give you a list of customers that meet certain criteria, like 'Let me know of all those customers who use *Windows* and own a business graphics product and have at least one hundred PCs on site.'" *PC Week* magazine produced thirty thousand names from their subscription list that met SPC's criteria. "We were able to formulate our request in such a way as to have a very focused and targeted marketing program for our new product."

The $22,500 campaign generated nine thousand qualified sales leads at a cost of about $2.50 per lead, compared with about $50 for the standard lead generated by a print ad. More than 13 percent of the targeted market elected to delay the purchase of a competitive business graphics product and wait for *Harvard Graphics for Windows.*

PRODUCT-ORIENTED ADVERTISING

Software Publishing spends an estimated $5 million a year advertising its wares in the computer press. About 85 percent of the ads are product-oriented and about 15 percent are corporate image advertising. That ratio of product ads will decrease in the next few years as Software Publishing grows "to a multi-hundred-million company. And to get there, we need to build a high level of trust. If customers are going to bet their business on your products, they want to know they can trust you."

FACING A FRAGMENTED MARKET

The fragmented nature of the PC software industry challenges SPC in many ways. SPC must reach a variety of different-size companies in a variety of different locations. It's quite impossible to make a personal sales call on every personal computer owner. "On an increasing basis, it's important that we follow up on sales leads from reader service card responses from our computer press advertising, seminar and trade show leads, and select databases. They've all been a crucial element in cost-effectively reaching the customer."

Software Publishing keeps a tight focus on the computer trade shows it selects. Trade shows can be prohibitively expensive. Companies have been known to spend hundreds of thousands of dollars on booths without clear results. "If you've truly got a new product and you've received good preshow press, then it's worth going to." To maximize returns, SPC makes sure it gets the biggest bang for its buck at a trade show. "There are many cost-effective ways to be present at a show, such as exhibiting in your strategic partners' booths or holding special previews and demonstrations of your new product. We let the Microsofts and IBMs blow the big bucks at the shows and we ride on their shoulders."

PLAYING FOR KEEPS WITH CUSTOMERS

Attracting customers is one thing, keeping them is another. To stay close to the customer, SPC has launched the following:

- A fax-on-demand program that allows anyone with a touch-tone phone and a fax machine to order a fax from the SPC library of technical tips and step-by-step technical procedures as well as literature on any SPC product.

- An order-by-fax program through which a customer is almost immediately faxed a product order form. The customer faxes back the form, and it's then entered into the system for quick delivery.

- "Auto-expert," a troubleshooting telephone program that helps customers with problems via an interactive voice-response machine. Auto-expert asks customers about their problem. Customers answer with their touch-tone phone. The program arrives at a solution based on the customer's responses. The customers can listen to the solution over the phone or request to have it faxed to them.

- *TechJournal,* the company's new bimonthly, customer-targeted magazine that highlights the various capabilities of SPC's software products. An annual subscription is $49.

SPC measures the success of its customer service through opinion polls and satisfaction surveys on its customer service and technical support line. "We do them every six months and results help us answer two important questions: What do we have to do to get better? And if we can do it better, how do we do it relative to our competition?"

PARLAYING VISIBILITY INTO SALES

One of the most important elements of the marketing mix at SPC is Gibbons himself. A Harvard M.B.A. who co-founded the company in 1980 at the age of thirty, the outspoken Gibbons has always maintained a high profile in Silicon Valley. As he explains, "I guess it all started with Steve Jobs. He brought high-tech into Hollywood. Then you have guys like Microsoft's Bill Gates being the richest guy in America. There's a lot of national interest in the people behind high-technology. It's a new part of the marketing mix. Executive visibility helps build credibility around a company. Therefore, we've all polished up our shoes, put on a new suit and we're out there giving the pitch. In general, I do between one and three speeches a month at important industry venues. I'd say my appearances generate leads for our sales organization. Positions and strategies that I articulate are often picked up by the press and some of our astute, leading-edge customers have found us that way."

When given a choice between speaking before an industry gathering or a meeting of SPC customers, such as a user's group, Gibbons opts for the customer groups. Software Publishing continues to give its customers what they want by keeping a tight focus on marketing fundamentals.

WORKING THE CHANNELS

Software Publishing distributes its products through a nationwide network, or channel, of forty-five hundred computer resellers, such as Egghead and Corporate Software. Software Publishing's channel sales group assists the resellers in managing their inventory of SPC products as well as helping them sell, promote, and merchandise the products. That group is responsible for about 70 percent of the company's sales.

The remaining 30 percent of the company's sales is managed by SPC's major accounts organization, which works closely with corporate end users and managers of a company's information services department. Reaching those key corporate decision makers is critical because corporations typically standardize one brand of software for an application like business presentations. When that happens, the software marketer wins an entire community of users with a single sale. "As our products have become more of a corporate standard, we've switched our selling and marketing strategies to focus more on the corporate decision makers. Then we follow up by generating broad, end user demand through our marketing communications. We want to get people to ask for the product."

INTERNATIONAL INROADS

In Europe, where SPC's sales are growing rapidly, Gibbons says the company relies almost entirely on resellers. "The reseller channel is more self-sufficient than it is in the United States. They even do the national accounts-type work that our corporate group would do here. They support our products, they take support calls, they make the corporate calls as well as do the retail push. They're substantially more vigorous and self-sufficient in marketing the product. They need less of our help."

In the company's second quarter of 1992 alone, 40 percent of the company's sales were overseas and Gibbons expects that half the company's sales will be international within two years. "There are big opportunities overseas because the competition is less intense. You still need a good organization over there, but yes, it's easier pickings over there."

SPC's products are represented by independent resellers in twenty countries, including the United Kingdom, France, Belgium, and Spain and a number of countries in Latin America and the Pacific Rim. International sales offices are located in Canada, the UK, Australia, the Netherlands, Belgium, Germany, Sweden, France, and Italy. SPC products are available in such languages as German, French, Canadian French, Finnish, Swedish, Spanish, Italian, Portuguese, and Dutch.

STRIKING THE RIGHT PRICE

Software Publishing has a two-pronged pricing strategy. *Harvard Graphics* is the premier product in the industry, and SPC charges a premium price for it.

In entrenched markets where SPC is not the leader, such as the database market or the drawing market, SPC uses a low-ball, gain-share strategy. The company's margins are typically break even on those products where SPC's trying to penetrate an entrenched market price. The margins for *Harvard Graphics,* however, are in the 30 to 40 percent range.

The surest way to build margins is to "build the best-of-grade product. Your engineering team and your marketing team have to be a jump ahead of the other guys in terms of new features and creative ideas and concepts. Our secret is that we execute best-of-grade new products and faster new product cycle times than the competition. Then you hustle hard to get the press and convince them that you have the best-of-grade product. Inventiveness is very important; you have to be inventive."

I truly believe you capture share of market share by capturing share of mind.

—DENNIS COLLINS,
MARKETING MANAGER OF TRUEVISION, INC.

One of the joys of pioneering a new technology is that you own the market—at least for a while. With its sophisticated computer circuit boards, Truevision helped create such markets as desktop video and computerized graphic arts. "Our challenge is to go from being the only show in town to being the best show in town."

Truevision's video boards transformed personal computers into special-purpose, high-performance videographics systems, and television news departments snapped them up to overlay titles and graphics on videotape. Film studios create razzle-dazzle special visual effects with them. The audiovisual departments of leading corporations use the boards to execute colorful video business presentations. Cosmetic surgeons use the technology to visualize scientifically their handiwork. Architects can prepare almost-true-to-life renderings of what planned buildings will look like by plugging Truevision's hardware into their PCs.

Truevision's video boards allow users to capture and manipulate video or photographic images for a variety of visual applications such as animation, 3-D modeling and rendering, sales presentations, and interactive point-of-sale displays. Creating such blue smoke and mirrors had been prohibitively expensive; closed-end videographics systems cost between $15,000 and $40,000. But by equipping a personal computer with a Truevision video board—which begins at about $1,000—graphic artists can achieve the results at a fraction of the cost of a dedicated videographic machine.

If it all sounds like multimedia—one of the hottest areas in personal computing—it is. Multimedia incorporates sound, animation, graphics, and video on a desktop or even a laptop computer. The world has Truevision to thank for a good part of it.

COMPETITION REARS ITS HEAD

Now, the Indianapolis-based company must guard against becoming a victim of its own success. "When I started with Truevision in 1985," recalls Cathleen Asch, the company's chief executive, "people would ask me who our competition was. Who were we selling against? I'd say, 'Well, we really don't have any competition.' And they'd say 'C'mon, that's a joke.' But it really wasn't because what we were doing was displacing a lot of specialized, higher-end systems with our integrated, board-level product. Nobody else was doing that at the time." Between 1985 and 1989 we faced very limited, sporadic competition. But by about 1990 people saw this whole area of video on the desktop developing into multimedia on the desktop."

Truevision faced competitors coming from both hardware and software. To cope with the new cast of competitors, Truevision's pricing strategy became aggressive. "We're usually at the higher end on price," Asch reports. "We obviously like good margins." But Truevision also knows that prices must be competitive with rivals.

CAPITALIZING ON A TRACK RECORD

Before the videographic market became flooded with competitors, Truevision wisely established the industry standards and a brand name product—Targa—that's become an almost generic description of the videographic process—a "Xerox" of videography. The Targa series of color graphics enhancement boards remains the most popular videographics product for IBM or IBM-compatible PCs. Truevision also has a line of boards that operate on Apple Macintoshes.

Armed with such strong brand identity, Truevision will prosper on a more competitive playing field driven by multimedia's intense popularity. Truevision likes to say that it was multimedia before multimedia was hot. Now, Truevision has established a reputation for quality and longevity in a relatively new field. With the field maturing, the sales volume of multimedia products is much higher. Truevision emphasizes its track record in its sales pitches and marketing messages, appealing to people who don't want to be left stranded two years from now when competitors whose eyes are focused more on the initial public offering (IPO) than the product fail. Truevision has a family of products so that a customer can get on board at whatever stage he or she wants. It's not just a single-product company.

STRONG LINK TO CUSTOMERS

Truevision has enjoyed a strong link between its engineers and its customers. The customers report what features they are seeking in a board, which is how Targa evolved. "The customers want more from us and we're listening. We'll try to get them what they want."

The company's reputation notwithstanding, Truevision's marketing will have to stay creative to continue posting 20 to 22 percent gains in revenues and profits each year. Solution selling—combining a Truevision board with software or hardware to solve a videographics problem for an end user—is growing. Joint marketing ventures will also be more common. "It's becoming tougher and tougher to go it alone in this kind of environment."

NO LONGER THE ONLY SHOW IN TOWN

To sustain its dominance in the industry, Truevision continues to build on its network of more than three hundred third-party software developers that develop applications that run on Truevision's video boards. It established a Developer Marketing Group specifically to cultivate working relationships with software manufacturers. "We've been able to harness the collective brain power of hundreds of software developers, which in turn has allowed us to concentrate on our hardware," Collins explains. "We could never have done that if we were locked into making a proprietary, turnkey system that integrated the software, hardware, and peripherals." Truevision figures the more software applications on the market that run on its video boards, the more it'll sell.

ROOTS IN AT&T

Truevision was founded in 1984 by eight computer graphics engineers as the Electronic Photography and Imaging Center (EPICenter), an intrapreneurial venture of AT&T. Three years later, the unit's twenty-eight employees engineered a $10 million buyout from AT&T and rechristened their venture Truevision. In 1992, Truevision became a wholly owned subsidiary of RasterOps, a Santa Clara, California–based computer graphics company. Truevision, which employs more than a hundred people, does not release its financials, but says its revenues are "in the eight figures."

While it was still known as EPICenter and under AT&T's wing, the venture was under some pressure by the parent company to focus only on creating a turnkey videographics system. Had the engineers caved in, Truevision probably wouldn't be doing the kind of co-marketing that's fueled its success and become the hallmark of their corporate strategy.

TAPPING THREE HUNDRED ADDITIONAL CHANNELS

Truevision approaches co-marketing from several angles. Among its major co-marketing ventures are the following.

Software manufacturers. In essence, the three hundred-plus software programs that run on Truevision's boards create more than three hundred additional distribution channels for Truevision boards. The company, which does not market itself directly to consumers, sells through more than four hundred dealers in the United States.

The company's sales force consists of fifteen independent sales agents that sell in three geographic regions. Each region has two Truevision sales managers to supervise the accounts. Truevision also sells in Western Europe, Asia, and Latin America through two international distributorships. About a third of the company's sales are international. By 1995, foreign sales should comprise about half the company's sales.

Software developers that strike strategic alliances with Truevision get plenty in return. Their product is listed in the annual software catalog of Truevision-compatible products that ships with every board. Truevision alerts its dealer base about the product. "We're bringing a ready channel of distribution to these developers so they can concentrate on the software and then pump it right into our channel."

Video production. Truevision joined forces with the AT&T Graphics Software Lab in Indianapolis and Diaquest, a Berkeley, California–based maker of a hardware board, to control a videotape deck used by studios to produce a video production package called the *Suite Deal.* The complete package allows video specialists to do high-resolution animation or titling overlays.

Joint venture. In *Director's Package,* Truevision teamed up with Marcomind Paracomp, a San Francisco–based software maker for the Macintosh, to create a high-quality video production package. Built for Truevision's NuVista+ board for the Macintosh, the package was jointly marketed through a special promotion that featured a videotaped demonstration. Inside the package, which featured a director shouting through a megaphone, users found a miniature megaphone with the companies' logos emblazoned on it.

"Both companies went on the road and trained dealers as well as trained end users with seminars. It married two companies which in turn focused on a single solution. The product has done wonderfully. The package took their dealer channel and our dealer channel, which had some overlap, and made them both stronger by giving them a common script and a common demo to show. The dealers were telling their customers: 'Hey, these two products create a solution.'"

Trade show alliances. Truevision's ecumenical spirit spills over into its trade show marketing. "Early on, we would typically turn over 50 to 70 percent of our booth space at trade shows to third-party developers." For example, if Truevision were exhibiting at a medical imaging show, it would invite into its booth companies that specialize in medical imaging software that use Truevision products to do demonstrations. "At a twelve-hundred-square-foot booth, we might turn over six demonstration stations to third-party people and only keep two or three stations for ourselves."

The smaller companies, which could not normally afford such space at a trade show on their own, appreciate Truevision "paying for the parking space," as Collins puts it. Partnering with smaller companies at trade shows also allows Truevision to command a greater presence on the trade show circuit. "We can cast a larger shadow"—a perception that's critical to an up-and-coming company, explains Collins.

To further make its presence known at trade shows, Truevision asks companies that use its videographics boards to display small acrylic tents atop computer monitors in their booths proclaiming "We use Truevision videographics products." When high-profile companies like Sony, JVC, or NEC show the Truevision flag, the company's presence looms even larger at a trade show.

CREATING BARRIERS THROUGH ADVERTISING

That "cast-a-large-shadow" theory applies to Truevision's computer and business press advertising that tops $1 million a year. Collins borrowed that strategy from McDonald's and Sara Lee, two accounts he handled when he worked at an advertising agency. "Being a smaller peripheral maker, we had to be careful about larger companies looking at the videographic market as an opportunity. If they saw no loud, clear leader they might feel they could just walk right in and dominate. Our ambitious advertising budget also kept the garage shops from nipping away at us because for them to outshout us in the marketplace, they'd have to spend beyond what they could afford. We created a barrier against both the small companies and the large companies who might feel they could jump in and crush us."

MARKETING AN EVENT

Truevision also keeps itself top of mind in the videographics community through the Truevision Videographics Contest, a nationwide competition that attracts nearly one thousand entries. Until recently, the computer artists would compete for a jackpot of $250,000.

Fearing the event was becoming too commercialized, Truevision scrapped the cash award. Now the company commissions an artist to create a classy-looking award that's presented to the winners each summer at the Special Interest Group on Graphics show. From there, Truevision takes the show on the road displaying the winners in about a dozen cities, providing the artists with unbeatable exposure.

The event has successfully captured the attention of art and creative directors at advertising agencies as well as computer, graphics, and even fine artists. "It's been a great way to show the world the advantages of computer-generated art," says Collins.

═══════════════════════════

> *Sometimes, I sit back and think, "What really is marketing?" If it's advertising, we're doing very little of that.*
>
> —ROBERT E. DOERING,
> PRESIDENT OF SULLIVAN DENTAL PRODUCTS

For seven years, Robert Sullivan traveled the Upper Midwest selling dental supplies out of his van. Along the way, he learned that dentists want two things: low prices and fast service. As a one-man road show, Sullivan could deliver both. But as his business grew—from the Sullivan Mobil Dental Supply van to a $100 million nationwide distributor known as Sullivan Dental Products, the challenge took on added complexity.

Thanks to an ingenious, yet simple inventory system, a team of dental assistants-turned customer service reps, and the creation of new national distribution centers, the Milwaukee-based company successfully spread its wings without sacrificing its trademark next-day delivery.

"It's comforting for the dentist to know that we can deliver products or equipment to them so quickly," explains Sullivan, the chairman and CEO of the West Allis, Wisconsin–based company he launched in 1980 and took public ten years later. "We've reached the point where we can provide that kind of service all over the country."

Competitive prices are important, but it's prompt delivery that truly sets Sullivan Dental apart from the hundreds of companies slugging it out in the $2 billion dental supplies business, explains Robert Doering, the company's president and chief operating officer. "If we get the order by three P.M., the dentist will have it by the next day. They love that kind of service." Sullivan provides next-day or, in a few cases, second-day delivery from three distribution centers. One near San Francisco serves eleven western states, the company's primary distribution center near Milwaukee serves the Midwest and South, and the newest center outside of Baltimore handles orders in fifteen northeastern states.

DIFFERENTIATING YOUR SERVICE

"In the service business, our competition sells the same products at about the same price, so obviously we have to do things very differently." Dental supplies are typically sold either through mail order or by companies with sales representatives assigned to a territory, but Sullivan Dental Products falls somewhere in between. "We have a sales force with a complete product catalog and customer service representatives who accept orders over a toll-free line. But we don't have a mail-order business." The company sends the catalog to its customer base of more than twenty-five thousand dentists, who are also paid regular visits by the company's nationwide sales force. The catalog is no longer sent to noncustomer dentists because "a catalog without a sales representative didn't have much value." Sullivan Dental, whose sales and net income have been increasing at a 30 percent or better annual clip, uses overnight delivery services to get its products to the dentist's office. But there's more to it than that, says Doering. The secret to their speedy delivery is simplicity.

QUICK AND SIMPLE

The backbone of the Sullivan distribution system is an alphanumeric code for each of the eight thousand products listed in its catalog, which makes filling an order as easy as looking for a library book on a shelf. The computerized code system allows the company's twenty customer service representatives to memorize about 90 percent of the product codes. The system appeals to customers, who don't need to know cumbersome product codes or even have a catalog handy. All they need to know is the name of the product.

The bulk of the company's business comes via its toll-free phone lines. The company's customer service reps, who are much more than just order takers, field the calls. "They're all former dental assistants who are used to working chairside with a dentist. They're very sensitive to a dentist's needs. Most of them came to us looking for a career change."

The customer service reps are intimately involved with the sales and distribution process. They attend sales meetings where marketing goals and objectives are outlined by company management, and they know their way around the company's warehouses. Sullivan

Dental experimented with telemarketing but scrapped that marketing practice after concluding it was too hard to reach and sell the dentist over the telephone.

In 1991, each of the customer service reps handled more than $3 million worth of business, which explains why Sullivan invests so much attention and training on them. The company pays more than just lip service to the concept of customer service.

Reps Come to Sell—Not Wheel and Deal

Drumming up sales in the field are 175 sales reps, armed with the company's two-hundred-page catalog, who visit customers regularly to demonstrate products and help the dentists and their staff understand the latest techniques in the dental profession. The prices in the catalog firmly establish the company's charges, relieving the sales rep of the need to wheel and deal on costs and allowing him or her to concentrate on providing value-added services and advice to the customer. "A good sales rep develops that kind of bond with the doctor." The company's field reps channel back to headquarters suggestions or concerns of the dentists.

Sullivan is not a training ground for sales reps in the dental products and equipment field, either. Many of the Sullivan sales reps have been seasoned selling for Sullivan's competitors. "The dental supplies industry is a $2 billion a year business, which is growing about 4 to 5 percent a year. But for us to continue growing 30 to 40 percent a year, we are going to have to grow at someone else's expense."

One way of doing that is attracting sales reps away from the competition. Selling for a company perceived to be on its way to more sizable share of market and above-the-industry compensation is a large part of the allure, but the company is "very, very careful about recruiting. We won't raid a competitor's sales staff. It's illegal and unethical. We don't want to put other people out of business."

Acquiring Good Reps

Sullivan also adds to its growing stable of sales representatives through acquisition of smaller competitors. In 1991, for example, Sullivan acquired dental supply companies in Grand Rapids, Michigan; San Jose, California; and Saugerties, New York.

A company that stakes its reputation so firmly on getting things to its customers in a hurry can't afford to be left shorthanded by its vendors. Sullivan, which does not manufacture any of the products or equipment it sells, insures itself against being left high and dry by carefully selecting about two hundred suppliers. No single vendor provides more than 7 percent of the products sold. Products that fail to generate strong interest by the customers are dropped from the inventory. These steps eliminate the need to explain surprises to customers.

About 80 percent of what the company sells is products, such as paper cups, cotton wads, filling material, and small equipment, according to Doering. The company also sells, installs, and services dental equipment through its fifteen sales and service centers scattered throughout the United States. Although the equipment side of the business contributes only 20 percent of the company's revenues, it is growing more rapidly than the products side. The centers, which are essentially small showrooms for dental equipment, are staffed with trained dental equipment specialists. Sullivan also has sixteen designers who assist dentists with the layout of their offices. "I think the dentists appreciate all the services that we can offer them," says Doering.

No matter how the word is getting around, Doering is confident that Sullivan Dental will capture a 10 percent share of the dental supply market in the next three years. "With a 4 or 5 percent share of the market, that means there's the potential for another 95 or 96 percent share of the market."

As a service company, our mission is to help our customers improve their productivity. We have to understand every phase of their business if we want to point out problems that could shut down or slow their production.

—W. Steven Weeber,
group vice president of Nalco Chemical Company

The notorious fifty-five-gallon drums, the environmental time bombs littering the nation's landfills, are history at Nalco Chemical

Company. Environmentally more conscious and fearful of liability, companies told Nalco they no longer wanted their chemicals shipped in drums.

Nalco was happy to adapt its products to the changing tastes of its customers. A maker of specialty chemicals—primarily to treat water at commercial and industrial sites—Nalco discontinued the drums in favor of a high-tech chemical storage system called Porta-Feed. Chemicals are now shipped in reusable four hundred-gallon stainless steel containers that are refilled when electronic sensors send a signal to Nalco. "The customer drove us out of the drum," explains John Berthoud, Nalco's corporate marketing director. "Customers are the driving force at this company. Our motto has always been: 'Finding the customer need and filling it.'"

Nalco has adopted several key steps to stay true to its motto of filling customers' needs:

- A three thousand-member sales force, all of whom have degrees in scientific specialties, spends about half its time in customers' plants, either monitoring the chemicals they've sold or serving on the customers' quality action teams.

- Each of the company's top twenty-two corporate officers, many of whom have risen though the sales and marketing ranks, individually manages a handful of key accounts.

- Managers in each of the company's 160 U.S. sales districts identify customers to be interviewed for up to an hour over the phone or in person by an outside consultant to measure customer satisfaction. To boost participation, Nalco reps contact the customers to encourage them to take part.

- The Total Quality Management (TQM) program diagnoses and solves problems not only at Nalco but at customer companies as well. The program is designed to give Nalco sales reps the expertise to serve on their customers' quality action teams.

QUEST FOR QUALITY

The push for customer-driven quality at Nalco, a $1.3 billion outfit, isn't magnanimous. Ruthlessly cost-conscious customers have been reducing their roster of suppliers, sometimes settling on a sole supplier. Nalco competes against the likes of DuPont and Dow Chemical and doesn't want to be left out in the cold when a company begins slashing away at its list of suppliers. "One reason that companies are dropping suppliers is simply a matter of time," explains W. Steven Weeber. "Managing suppliers is a lot of work. The other reason is that many suppliers can't live up to the quality standards of their client companies."

To adapt, Nalco launched a companywide quality management program designed to imbue every employee with the principles of such quality gurus as W. Edwards Deming and Philip Crosby. Nalco's quest for quality hasn't been lost on its customers.

SEEKING PREFERRED STATUS

"We win a lot of 'select' or 'preferred' supplier awards from such key customers as Alcoa or Campbell Soup. When you're one of as many as ten thousand suppliers for a company, that's quite an honor." The return on Nalco's investment in quality has been encouraging. The company's growing reputation for high-quality products and service translated to an estimated $40 million in new business in 1991. Over the past five years, the company's sales have grown 65 percent and profits have nearly doubled to $131 million.

The Naperville, Illinois–based company, founded in 1928, initially provided chemicals to treat water used in industrial boilers and steam locomotives. The company has since grown into the world's largest marketer of waste-water chemicals with more than forty ventures worldwide. About 40 percent of the company's revenues are from overseas, where Nalco helps companies meet both water and air quality standards. Nalco began making quality its battle cry in the mid-1980s. That's when Weeber returned from Paris, where he headed the company's fast-growing European operations. "The quality movement in the United States was quite apparent to me. We decided at that point we wanted to institute our own Total Quality Management program." To underscore Nalco's quality message, the company produced a twenty-page magazine titled *Partners in Quality—Nalco and You*, which was distributed to Nalco's customers and prospects and which explains the company's Quali-Trak program and profiles a cross-section of the company's employees.

THE BEST OF TIMES, THE WORST OF TIMES

The TQM effort was launched at a critical time for the company. Nalco generates the bulk of its revenues by making and supplying specialty chemicals to help industries purify the water in their heating and cooling systems as well as in the manufacturing process. For example, Nalco makes a chemical that allows paper mills to wash impurities out of the pulp. The company's profit margin of a little more than 10 percent is typical of the specialty chemical business, which enjoys 4 to 5 percent higher margins than the commodity chemical industry (chlorine, caustic soda, benzene, etc.). Nalco caters to niche markets and makes specialty chemicals for dozens of other basic industries such as steel, food service, petroleum, mining, and metalworking. Unfortunately, many of those key industries began to contract in the face of stiffer economic competition in the 1980s, and Nalco felt the pinch.

At the same time, however, a growing sense of environmentalism began to sweep the country. Many companies turned to Nalco to help them meet federally mandated air and water emission standards. Nalco wisely repositioned itself as an environmental company through the development of more water treatment, air pollution control, and waste minimization systems. It convened special task forces to look at the impact of the Clean Air Act and the Clean Water Act. An example is Fuel Tech, a joint venture with a British company to create air pollution control technology enabling manufacturers to reduce smog-forming nitrogen oxide emissions from their boilers or furnaces by up to 70 percent.

THE WATER DOCTORS

Carrying Nalco's solution-oriented, environmental message to the marketplace is its three thousand salespeople. Their degrees are put to good use. "They not only must understand our business but the customer's as well. As a service company, our mission is to help our customers improve their productivity. We have to understand every phase of their business if we want to point out problems that could shut down or slow their production."

Like any savvy business-to-business marketer, Nalco's sales force does much more than sell. "Our reps serve on customers' quality action teams." Although all of Nalco's six thousand employees undergo quality training, the sales force must complete a second more intensive level of training, called Quali-Trak II. The training, conducted by both the company's in-service training staff and outside quality consultants, prepares the reps to serve on a customer company's quality action team.

"Nalco has no regrets about the time our reps spend on these quality teams because it further cements the doctor-patient relationship. Some customers refer to the Nalco reps as "the water doctors." "We put our salespeople on a pedestal, because in our customers' minds our reps are Nalco," says Weeber.

REDUCING SALES FORCE TURNOVER

Any company that relies so heavily on its sales force to carry its marketing message must guard against high turnover in the sales ranks. "We were not happy about the former level of turnover in our sales force—about 15 percent a year." That's not unusually high by industry standards, but Nalco wanted it much lower. Customers like dealing with a familiar sales rep.

To get to the root of the problem, Nalco conducted in-depth surveys with its worldwide sales force. "We were fried in the survey on the quality of our sales managers." To support that level, Nalco decided to do much more training of its front-line sales managers to make them more sensitive to the people working for them. The message was, "We don't like turnover. We're tired of seeing people leave for not very good reasons. We can't achieve our quality goals if you're grinding your people out."

Analysis of exit surveys further revealed that sales reps were leaving for four primary reasons: lack of compensation, heavy work loads, lack of recognition, and lack of advancement. To address the sales reps' frustrations over a perceived lack of advancement, Nalco created a "dual ladder, which tells them in essence, 'You don't have to be the boss. It's okay to be a sales rep because if you're a good one, you'll be rewarded.'"

Nalco's twenty-two corporate officers have a natural affinity to its sales force. Not only did nearly all of them rise from the sales or marketing ranks but each of them continues to sell to the company's key accounts. Weeber, for example, makes regular visits to Alcoa,

BASF, and DuPont, which, curiously, is both customer and competitor. "When I go out, I learn firsthand what we're doing right and wrong."

TIGHTENING TIES TO THE CUSTOMER

Another way Nalco makes it hard for customers to turn their backs on them is through its innovative just-in-time delivery system known as Chem-Call. Electronic sensors in the stainless-steel containers automatically alert Nalco to when it's time to deliver another shipment of chemicals to the plant site. Traditionally, customers had to monitor the levels themselves. "It's another way that we as a supplier can enhance our relationship with a customer," explains Ali D. Ata, Nalco's manager of corporate marketing systems. "The computerized tracking system also lets our reps analyze a customer's use of chemicals."

The new delivery system is also kinder on the environment. The chemicals are now delivered to a customer's plant in returnable two hundred- or four hundred-gallon Porta-Feed stainless steel containers that all but eliminate the risk of a spill at a customer's plant.

FLUSHED BY THE MARKETPLACE

Ironically, the Porta-Feed success story arose from one of Nalco's biggest marketing failures. The original program was launched in the 1970s but was scrapped after the marketplace failed to accept it—the time just wasn't right. "One of the biggest problems was that customers weren't returning the Porta-Feeds to be refilled and we didn't have a system to keep track of them."

In this more environmentally conscious age, the marketplace has taken to the advanced chemical handling system. "The technology is more advanced and the management is completely behind the program this time." Customers pay a premium for the Porta-Feeds, but convenience and reduction of environmental liability outweigh concerns over the price.

Redemption of the Porta-Feed program serves as a valuable marketing lesson. "We sat down and listed all the mistakes we made the first time and figured out a way to avoid them a second time. This time it worked."

We're well positioned for continued strong growth because we operate at the intersection of telecommunications and computers. We think it's a wonderful place to be.

—DOUGLAS CHANCE,
PRESIDENT AND CEO OF OCTEL COMMUNICATIONS

Competing against telecommunications powerhouses like AT&T and Northern Telecom would seem to be the major marketing challenge to voice mail systems maker Octel Communications. But Douglas Chance, Octel's president and CEO, says the company's marketing mission is much more difficult than that. "It's getting people to try the concept of voice mail. Even a year ago people were irritated if they were instructed to leave a message on someone's voice mail," he says. "Today, they're upset if there's no voice mail box to leave a message. There's been a major social change."

Stories about managers uprooting their company's voice mail equipment because "they were tired of their employees hiding behind the systems" are appearing less often in the media. Chance is a twenty-four-year veteran of Hewlett-Packard and took the top job at Octel in 1990. The ten-year-old Milpitas, California–based company now has a 22 percent and growing share of the voice mail market.

To further drive corporate America's acceptance of voice mail and its various applications, Octel aggressively educates the marketplace through nearly forty customer seminars a year. These are videotaped testimonials of satisfied corporate customers that Octel sends to five hundred of the *Fortune* 1000 CEOs. Octel even holds joint seminars with competitors—all agree to hold the company sales pitches in favor of a pitch for voice mail technology itself.

VOICE MAIL AS A LABOR-SAVING DEVICE

A key marketing message Octel conveys is improved productivity. Although U.S. manufacturing productivity has grown by about 30 percent in the last ten years, gains on the white collar side have been a relatively anemic 10 percent during that same time. The solution to better productivity in the office is the phone, an important nexus in the exchange of information. "What could be simpler than the keypad on a telephone? We think of it as a computer terminal and its printer is a fax machine," says Rob Reid, vice president of marketing.

While Octel primes the marketplace with accounts of improved productivity and ease of use, its technological breakthroughs have allowed it to keep a leg up on the competition despite their greater financial, technical, and sales resources. In 1991, Octel sold $160 million worth of voice mail equipment versus the $120 million of voice mail systems sold by AT&T, its nearest competitor. In 1992, the company expects sales to top $200 million. Octel has been growing between 30 and 40 percent a year. Profit margins are healthy—ranging between 12 and 15 percent, according to Chance. Octel's customers include more than forty companies in the *Fortune* 100 industrial group, including General Electric, Amoco, and Hewlett-Packard. Octel targets small, medium, and large companies, although it's done best with larger companies because they're better able to afford a leading-edge technology such as voice processing.

Another key segment are the seven Regional Bell Operating Companies, or the Baby Bells, such as Ameritech or Pacific Telesis. The Baby Bells became customers after a 1987 federal court ruling that allowed them to offer services like voice mail to residential and business customers. Fortunately for Octel, the ruling barred the Baby Bells from making the voice mail systems. Octel has been more than happy to develop and supply the equipment.

A More Versatile System

One reason Octel has been able to outsell Ma Bell is because AT&T's Audix voice mail system is compatible only with its own equipment. Octel, however, can sell to a broader market because its voice mail systems are compatible with eighty-three different telephone systems. One of the company's newest products, Powercall, allows telephone users to access personal computers and fax machines from remote locations. The technology turns a touch-tone telephone into a voice and information workstation by integrating voice, image, and data media. For example, a sales manager could access the company's database to determine inventory levels, receive product information, request that a copy of the latest promotional notice from marketing be sent to his or her fax machine, or leave a message with the sales force via voice mail. Powercall has valuable external uses such as allowing customers or vendors to tap into the company's database and receive information via voice or fax.

REACHING THE DECISION MAKERS

The systems don't sell themselves. Octel uses several important marketing tools including:

- Direct mail.

- Telemarketing.

- Target marketing.

- Videotaped customer testimonials.

- Seminars.

Octel outsources its direct mail and telemarketing to service bureaus. Reference, or word-of-mouth, selling is also a key ingredient in the company's marketing mix.

The company's sales, marketing, and customer support organization of nearly six hundred people is supplemented by independent distributors who sell in the United States and in such foreign markets as Canada, Australia, and Singapore. In Europe, Octel's products and services are sold by several of its wholly owned subsidiaries. International sales are growing rapidly and represent about 25 percent of the company's revenues.

Like many business marketers, Octel prefers targeted marketing to mass marketing. "We prefer to deal as directly as possible with our customers." For example, when Octel had a major product announcement, such as the Powercall rollout, the company invited its customers to twenty-two sites around the country. The 1990 announcement was carefully choreographed and included prerecorded film clips of the new product's applications. "For a high-technology company like us, it was a good way to demonstrate our technical expertise."

USING VIDEO MARKETING TECHNIQUES

Another tool is videoteleconference seminars that link Octel with a customer site. "The customers like it because they don't have to travel," Reid explains. "What's best, though, is that the sessions are interactive. Both parties can see each other, and can better interact through body language. It's an excellent training and selling tool, plus it exposes our managers to valuable feedback."

Octel also lets some of its customers market for them in the form of videotaped testimonials, which are sent to key customers and prospects. The videotapes have been used as both an introduction to Octel and as a way of reinforcing messages delivered in a sales call. Octel has twelve videotapes, all of which are industry specific. The videotaped testimonials are done in a television interview format, but they're never dull. Some customers are very enthusiastic. Octel will continue to explore other leading-edge electronic marketing tools because of the high-technology nature of many of its customers.

AT YOUR SERVICE

SERVICE COMPANIES are finding new ways to help corporations do everything from paying their employees to running their computers. Automatic Data Processing (ADP) helped launch the outsourcing movement more than forty years ago when it convinced a handful of companies that it could process their payrolls more efficiently and less expensively than they could. Today ADP issues more than five hundred million paychecks a year for a quarter of a million companies throughout the world.

Electronic Data Services (EDS) is to computer services as ADP is to payrolls. EDS sells companies on the idea of turning their computing over to them by "insinuating ourselves into every company business process," explains Barry Sullivan, EDS's director of marketing.

Devon Direct is not your traditional advertising agency concerned strictly with burnishing a company's corporate image or leading brands. Devon has become one of the nation's fastest-growing agencies by involving itself in the entire marketing process of its clients—from planning to pricing to positioning.

Centex Telemanagement has plenty of room to grow because it regards any company with a telephone as a potential new customer, reasons sales and marketing chief Carol Krane. Centex has won legions of new customers by helping them select the best telecommunications services available.

We will never try to develop a strategy that wins on price. There is nothing unique about pricing.

—JOSH S. WESTON, CHAIRMAN AND CEO
OF AUTOMATIC DATA PROCESSING, INC.

Operating one of the nation's largest computer processing and information services companies is like life in a fishbowl. "Our service is on display every minute of every day," explains Josh S. Weston, chairman and CEO of ADP.

The Roseland, New Jersey–based company is best known for handling the paychecks of more than twelve million Americans. If you're counting, that's more than five hundred million paychecks a year and some twenty million laser-printed W-2 forms. The company also provides computing and information services to nearly half the nation's auto dealers; claims services for eighteen of the nation's top twenty auto insurers; and record keeping, order entry, proxy services, and real-time stock quotations for 350 of the biggest U.S. financial institutions and stock brokerages. To say the least, it's a demanding clientele.

"Our kind of service has an ongoing, daily requirement for client service, client responsiveness. All you have to do is hiccup with the stock quotation service for five seconds and every client sees it. Payroll isn't every minute, but aside from delivering a payroll to an employer every week you get calls all over the spectrum every single hour of every single day and if you're not there to respond to their inquiries or calls, the fact that you delivered their payroll on time last week becomes irrelevant. If I bought a car, I wouldn't see anyone from the dealership for quite a while. What we market is a service, not a product, and our success or failure depends on the quality of the daily interfacing with that client."

The company's success has been phenomenal. ADP has chalked up record profits and revenues for more than forty consecutive years. The company can trace its success to several factors:

- The company has a three-tiered sales and services structure that strictly separates the sales function from the service function.

- In addition to financial data, ADP aggressively collects and analyzes service performance data to detect flaws or look for ways to better deliver service.

- ADP is almost fanatical about feedback from its customers. Each of its more than 230,000 customer companies is surveyed twice a year.

ADP's Chinese Wall

Conventional wisdom holds that the same person should be responsible for sales and service. ADP, however, recognized long ago that to make a single person responsible for sales and service would not work.

ADP's three-tiered approach starts with a sales representative, whose only job is to develop new clients. The new client is then passed off to an account executive whose mission is to shepherd the client through to the first day of processing. The account executive maintains a long-term relationship with the account, but it's the client-service rep, the final link in the chain, who'll provide the daily troubleshooting and service upgrades for the client.

In the company's Employer Services Division, for example, ADP maintains thirteen hundred sales representatives, five hundred account executives, and one thousand client-service representatives. Employer Services, the company's oldest and largest division, generates about 55 percent of the company's $1.8 billion in annual revenues.

"Salespeople are on the road all the time. We don't want our salespeople in the office," says Weston. "It wouldn't be the best use of their skills to convert a client to a higher-level system. We can understand that a client may have developed a preference for that salesperson. But if we do our job in separating the sales function from the service function, the client will feel comfortable with the service rep and no longer feel the need to talk to the field rep who isn't around anyway." If handled skillfully, the risk of miscommunication between the three tiers of employees in the sales and service realm is minimal.

Weston likens ADP's business to a layer cake. "In a repetitive business like ours, the height of the cake is the sum of all the previous layers. Each layer is one year's worth of new clients that our salespeople have brought in. It's the job of the rest of us to preserve the height of the cake."

Measuring Performance by the Numbers

ADP may be in the business of processing information, but it also collects plenty of it for its internal use. "It's not just financial data we collect like everyone else. We collect a great deal of client performance data that's circulated to our sales managers all over the country."

The information can serve as an early warning of a service breakdown. For example, ADP can move very quickly if there's a telephone answering problem in certain cities. Suppose the Kansas City office has been averaging scores of seventy-five for telephone answering for the past five months and then in one month falls to sixty. The manager ought to recognize the problem, but just in case he or she doesn't, the performance data will call that to his or her attention. The service performance data also allows managers to see how they are doing in terms of service compared with other managers around the country. The service indicators are also circulated so that it's clear to every sales and service rep how each manager is doing.

The Power of Peer Pressure

The comparative sales and service information has been used as the basis of peer group competition, peer group pressure, or as Weston put it more strongly, embarrassment. "But we prefer to stick to the positive and use the information to identify and reward our top performers."

Peer group competition has been a traditional way to stoke the engines of the Employer Services Division's sales force. Every Tuesday night, regional sales managers sit down with their troops. Each sales rep must give an accounting of the new business he or she has generated for the company in the last week. Weston explains that this isn't designed to be cutthroat. "We want everyone to recognize that there's foam rubber on the ground. We're not trying to kill anyone if they fall. The numbers are there to show people that there's an area where they have an opportunity to do better. If you're a pole vaulter and you see a competitor vaulting twenty feet and you're only going sixteen, you'll push yourself to find a way to get to twenty."

ADP Asks: "How Are We Doing?"

Another form of feedback is provided by the company's client surveys. ADP sends every client two surveys per year, or about forty thousand surveys each month, amounting to about one-sixth of ADP's entire clientele. An impressive 50% of them are returned to provide a reliable statistical barometer. "If you only survey your clients once a year you have to wait too long to find out how you're doing. We want a continuum of feedback." When the surveys come back to headquarters, they're broken down into regions, and each service representative receives a score. "Everybody knows how they're doing. They can see they're getting better and be proud about it. Or they're tipped off that the quality of their service is not as high as last month's."

An Argument for Outsourcing

Quality service is critical to a company like ADP, whose message to the marketplace is, "We are experts in certain businesses that are not really strategic to your business. We can do those functions more accurately, more efficiently, and less expensively than you can do it yourself. We're doing payrolls for over two hundred thousand companies and we have four hundred people in the Research and Development unit who are payroll experts. We're spreading the cost of four hundred programmers over two hundred thousand companies. A company trying to do it alone would require a couple of programmers.

"In the payroll area today, regrettably from the world's point of view, there are two thousand different regulatory authorities that impose income taxes. It's not just the IRS. Payrolls can be very complicated for companies that have a multiple state or multiple country presence." ADP derives about 6 percent of its annual revenues from international markets, handling payrolls in countries such as Canada, Brazil, the Netherlands, the UK, and Hong Kong. ADP was a pioneer in the field of outsourcing. Henry Taub, who founded the company in 1949 and who now serves as honorary chairman of the board, first persuaded employers to turn over their payroll work. The idea of letting another company handle something as sensitive as their payroll was considered very foreign at the time. Today, it's commonplace, although ADP still must sell itself to new clients.

Although ADP is the largest player in the payroll business today, there are more than one thousand companies that offer payroll services. The largest competitors are Paychex, Control Data, and, until recently, the Bank of America's Services Division, whose primary business is payroll processing. ADP bought the unit, which had been producing annual revenues of more than $125 million for about seventeen thousand clients. ADP plans to hire virtually all of the unit's employees.

COMMUNICATING THE MESSAGE

The message about the advantages of outsourcing is primarily delivered by ADP's sales force, whose efforts are supported through well-targeted advertising that relies to a great degree on direct mail. ADP gets the most mileage out of its direct mail by taking three steps:

1. Spending the extra money to buy highly qualified lists of prospects whose names and titles are current.

2. Sending prospects personalized letters that are laser printed on high-quality paper.

3. Including a postcard that invites a direct response, either by returning the postcard or by calling a toll-free number, which is processed by an outside service bureau.

ADP spends more than $5 million a year on direct mail; Employer Services is the biggest user. The highly targeted direct mail generates an exceptional 3 to 5 percent response rate—1 percent is considered a typical return. Half of those responses are eventually converted into sales.

ADP also spends about $3.5 million annually to reach decision makers through print advertising in trade journals, and each fall the Employer Services Division spends about $2 million to buy drive-time spots on news-oriented radio stations in forty-two markets. The radio campaign is run in the fall because that's when companies typically make decisions about their payroll for the next year. ADP does no corporate-level advertising and no television advertising.

Shunning Customer Discounts

ADP's prices tend to be "equal to or somewhat higher than what prevails among our competitors." As noted above, ADP never uses low prices as a marketing strategy. "We've refused to make our claim to fame that our services are lower priced, because anyone can match you on that kind of claim. We'd rather earn the full price than chase a company with a discounted price, and with an incomplete product and lousy service."

The combination of ADP's sales force persistence, strong marketing message, and continually growing reputation allows the company to command a premium in the marketplace.

Outsourcing is based on trust, and once you violate that trust, you're finished forever in the service business.

—Barry Sullivan, director of marketing
at Electronic Data Systems

While IBM was making a fortune by making computers, Ross Perot was quietly building a business not by building computers but by providing companies with computing services.

Now Big Blue—suddenly awash in red ink—is stealing a page from Electronic Data Systems, Perot's first and by far most successful company. In 1991, IBM organized a subsidiary, Integrated Systems Solutions Corporation, to manage other companies' computing needs. The process is called outsourcing and it's what EDS does best.

Not surprisingly, EDS executives greet IBM's entry into the computer services market with mixed emotions. "It will put our margins under some pressure," admits Barry Sullivan, EDS's director of marketing. "But when IBM comes into the market, it gives outsourcing the stamp of being a standard business practice. That's something that EDS could not do despite our successes. They sort of legitimize the practice and from that comes rapid revenue growth."

EDS may have a leg up on their new rival. With its experience, EDS knows that there's a whole lot more to being a service company than just declaring it. A lot of companies like IBM that have histori-cally sold products rather than services are changing. As Sullivan puts it, they're proclaiming "I just got religion. I am now a service company."

THE SERVICE MIND-SET

By now the story of Perot's founding of EDS for $1,000 is familiar to millions of Americans. In 1984, twenty-two years after founding EDS, Perot sold out to General Motors for $2.5 billion. Still a sub-sidiary of GM (although its stock is traded separately on the New York Stock Exchange as GME), EDS reported record earnings in 1991 of $565 million on revenues of $7.1 billion, another record.

The year 1991 also marked the first time since GM acquired EDS that revenues from sources outside of GM exceeded revenues derived from business with the financially troubled giant. About 53 percent of all EDS revenues come from contracts with organizations such as General Electric, Apple Computer, Kmart, and the city of Chicago. GM accounted for more than 80 percent of EDS's revenues in the years immediately after the deal.

Perot had run the button-down operation with an iron fist. He was a stickler on customer service, a legacy that lives on at Dallas-based EDS. The mind-set of a service company is radically different from that of a manufacturer. "When you sell a product, you don't want that cus-tomer to come see you again until he's ready to get a new one. As a service company, we want to insinuate ourselves into every company business process and be constantly bringing them new ideas and inno-vations to make their company better," says Sullivan.

"Our view is that a service company should be like an au pair where someone moves in with you, shares birthdays, and becomes very close. Our marketing secret is focus. By that I mean we focus on bringing benefits to the end user."

Under a typical outsourcing scenario, EDS signs long-term con-tracts with clients to take over and operate their data processing operations, buys the client company's computer hardware from the company itself, and hires the customer's data processing employees.

EDS also serves as a consultant to client companies or as a systems integrator, designing and installing complicated networks of hardware and software for its client companies.

Rich Vein of Opportunity

Outsourcing could prove to be the computing industry's mother lode in the 1990s. Information systems consultants estimate that as many as 50 percent of all major U.S. corporations are considering farming out their data processing. That could mean billions of dollars for the outsourcing industry, including EDS. The market is coming around to EDS's point of view on information technology. Companies are seeing it's less mainframe computers and glass boxes than it is a service. For this sea change, EDS has positioned itself superbly. In the 1990s, companies will return to the core competencies—sticking to what they do best. "That's fueled the phenomenon of outsourcing," Sullivan makes clear.

Stumbling Blocks

The biggest challenge EDS faces continues to be convincing prospective customers that it can manage their information technology more efficiently than they can. Some companies fear that by farming out their information services they're not only surrendering some of the best and brightest employees but signing away a critical element of their corporate persona. "We hear that argument all the time. Outsourcing is based on trust and once you violate that trust, you're finished forever in the service business," Sullivan continues. "We have this long trail of six thousand customers that we can point to as references. That alleviates some of the fear." Another challenge for EDS is assuring prospects that outsourcing is not irreversible. "Some companies ask, 'Is this like a vasectomy?'" Sullivan says with a laugh. "We assure them that if for any reason their business circumstances change and they want to do things differently, they can. We don't have many instances of giving a contract back. For example, we had Arrow Electronics. We didn't do as good a job in articulating the value of the services we were bringing them, and they decided to take it back." The divorce was amicable. "Arrow will go anywhere and at anytime to tell a wonderful story about how EDS went every extra mile to reverse the process."

MARKETING ITS SERVICES

EDS pursues a multifaceted marketing program that includes:

- A specialized sales force.

- Public appearances by more than one hundred of its executives at key information technology gatherings.

- Its first-ever corporate advertising campaign.

EDS's sales force of a little more than five hundred reps is spread relatively thinly across the company's thirty-eight divisions. "Our sales force, by most standards, is very modest," says Sullivan. "But a relatively small sales force lends itself to greater focus." Each of the "strategic business units" focuses on such vertical markets as government, health care, financial services, energy, retail, and insurance. Every division develops its own marketing strategy and is responsible for sales and profits. "The point is, we're organized around our customers' businesses." Although each division's customer profile is different, all EDS reps deliver one central message: EDS can create strategic value and strategic benefit through information technology.

RIDING THE SPEAKER CIRCUIT

That message is echoed by EDS executives and marketers who've taken to the stump frequently in recent years. Lester Alberthal, EDS's chairman, has established a more empowering style of leadership. Now more than one hundred people can speak for the company in a whole variety of forums. The newfound emphasis on appearing at and participating in information technology forums has built the company's image, which previously consisted of little more than Ross Perot's charismatic personality.

SELLING THE CUSTOMER'S SUCCESS

To reinforce its message, EDS spent an estimated $18 million in 1991 to launch its first-ever corporate advertising campaign. The campaign, which is continuing in 1992, includes ads in leading business press publications as well as spots on network and cable television.

The campaign does not tell the story of EDS's success but of its customers' success. For example, one print ad explains how EDS helped retailing giant Kmart achieve record profits in 1991. "They did it, in part, thanks to one of the world's most comprehensive, highly integrated point-of-sale bar coding and scanning systems," the ad proclaims. "Developed in partnership with EDS, it helps Kmart identify and respond to shifts in customer buying patterns with unprecedented speed and accuracy."

"The impression that we want this campaign to leave is that EDS focuses on the end user's benefit," says Sullivan, stating the truth, which is always the best advertising. "And unlike a lot of information technology advertising, which talks about megabytes, megahertz, gigabytes, and other mindless features, we're talking in a language that end users at a company can understand. You don't have to be technically educated to read our stuff. We want to create this spot in the target audience's mind that will separate us from everyone else by saying, 'We use information technology to create a business benefit. We don't sell information technology.'"

STRAIGHTFORWARD PRICING STRATEGY

Pricing strategies are left in the hands of the thirty-eight divisions, although the entire company follows a common approach to setting prices. "Our pricing strategies are pretty straightforward, and I'm not shy about talking about them," remarks Sullivan, who notes the relative chaos in pricing greatly increased competition has brought. "Any time new competitors come in, they bring discontinuities. Some don't know how to price. You have people who are pricing based on what they think is going to work. What we do is focus on the benefit to the customer. That is, we base our price on the value we create for the customer. For example, if what I'm offering you will improve a manufacturer's turn on inventory and that translates to $3.2 million, we will price it so that you will realize some of that and some of that is our compensation. If we took it all, there wouldn't be any value."

Because EDS adapts its pricing strategies to the value its service brings to a customer, the influx of new competitors into the market has not significantly influenced their pricing. The increased competi-

tion has, however, sharpened EDS's focus on its operating procedures. In short, EDS has become more competitive, and its marketing
more disciplined.

EDS will not lay off people to maintain its margins. Sullivan suc-
cinctly analyzes the effect of layoffs on morale. "You may be able to
afford to lay off people in a product business, but in a service business, it's your people who deliver the service and you want them to
feel they are part of the company. You want them to feel secure." EDS
has more than seventy thousand employees, a huge increase from
just eight years ago when it employed a mere thirteen thousand.

BULLISH ON THE INTERNATIONAL MARKET

EDS is parlaying its success in the United States into the international
markets, where it plans to derive 50 percent of its revenues by 1995.
"We call that a milestone, rather than a goal." To establish its beach-
head in Europe more firmly, EDS engineered the $272 million hostile
takeover of SD-Scicon, one of Europe's leading computer services
companies. The British-based company had a broad base of British
and French customers, and gave EDS a critical mass in Europe. "It
gave us more capability on the front end of our service continuum,"
notes Sullivan. "Most of our U.S. contracts are systems management
(outsourcing) contracts and they tend to be long-term contracts to
operate information technology on behalf of the customer. But it's in
consulting where you get the chance to identify new opportunities.
What the acquisition did was round out our service offering in
Europe."

EDS already has a presence in thirty countries and hopes to take
Europe by storm. "If we can develop a lot of customer success stories there, we can define the market." A problem is the fact that
European business leaders often don't have a clearly defined sense
of outsourcing. "They've read a little bit about it, but they don't
know the particulars about how it's carried out in the United
States." What Sullivan tells them is that EDS can help them close the
gap between a company's information technology equipment and
the performance it's capable of generating. "That's our primary
message. It's not that we're going to save you money." EDS is going
to make them money.

Generating a strong response is not that difficult. The challenge is creating a strong response rate that's sensitive to a client's bottom line. Profit performance is what really matters to a client.

—RON GREENE, CO-FOUNDER AND PRINCIPAL
OF DEVON DIRECT

Even though he's co-founder of one of the nation's fastest-growing advertising firms, Ron Greene says "traditional advertising is almost the last thing we'll consider doing for a client." That's because when Greene and partner Jim Perry sit down with a client or a prospect, their sights are more often focused on improving a company's cash flow or creating fresh business expansion opportunities. Their comprehensive approach sometimes catches clients off guard as they enmesh themselves in a client's entire marketing process from initial planning to research, pricing, and positioning.

Furthermore, when the talk turns to advertising, they're not talking about the kind of advertising that burnishes corporate images or brands. Rather, it's direct response, a form of advertising that solicits orders by mail or telephone. Advertisers have become increasingly fond of the technique because they know almost to the dollar how much each ad sells. Measurability is very important in advertising these days.

"Generating a strong response is not that difficult. The challenge is creating a strong response rate that's sensitive to a client's bottom line. Profit performance is what really matters to a client," explains Greene. Conventional advertising agencies, hell-bent on generating a big response without regard to a company's finances, do a disservice to their clients.

Taking a client for a ride is not Devon's style. Greene says they're looking for clients with whom they can be partners on a long-term basis, rather than the quick kill. Capitalized billings for the privately held Philadelphia-based firm now top $100 million, making it one of the nation's fastest-growing independent direct-response ad shops.

PEDDLING PORCELAIN PLATES

Ironically, Green and Perry never thought they'd be in the business of advising companies on more effective marketing. They launched the firm in 1983 to market porcelain plates and hand-painted sculptures directly to the homes of their customers.

They were both well prepared for this mission. They met at the Franklin Mint in Philadelphia where Greene served for seven years as vice president of advertising and marketing. Greene was among the architects of the Mint's successful metamorphosis from a coin minting operation into a highly diversified merchandising business and one of the nation's leading direct-marketing powerhouses. Perry was vice president of marketing in charge of product development at the Mint. "We both felt we were lucky to have found each other there," says Greene.

After launching their business, they began to field requests for advice from businesses that didn't have much experience with direct marketing, and it dawned on them that they could make a living at it. They eased their way out of marketing porcelains and into the business of marketing their direct response expertise. Devon's early customers included such high prestigious—and profitable—companies as Commodore Business Machines, American Express, *Commentary Magazine*, and the Numis Gallery, a marketer of home decor and gift items.

They developed a strategy of targeting an industry that could benefit from direct marketing. They zeroed in on the telecommunications industry, which was ripe for direct marketing in the wake of a federal judge's order that AT&T be broken up. Almost instantly, there was a fierce battle for the long-distance telephone customer. Greene and Perry recognized that MCI Communications would be a key player in that market battle.

"We pushed hard to land some business with MCI," Greene remembers. "Somehow, we got in the door through a lot of persistence and convinced them to try a high-volume direct-mail campaign. They were a new company, and willing to try something different. We said, 'You need to communicate your message into these residences in a very methodical way.' It was a big break for us, because it put us on the map in the telecommunications business. It's still one of our primary areas of expertise."

Devon's MCI campaign was a monumental undertaking that involved the distribution of more than 150 million personalized direct-mail packages to households and businesses across the nation during a twenty-two-month period beginning in 1984. For MCI, Devon put into place a first-of-its-kind neighborhood-by-neighborhood marketing plan that encouraged hundreds of thousands of residential customers to subscribe to MCI. Devon reached business customers through a combination of direct mail and sales calls by MCI reps.

PARLAYING ITS SUCCESS

Devon Direct's success with MCI caught the attention of US Sprint. In 1986, Sprint enlisted Devon to help position them in a drive to capture some of AT&T's market share. Devon Direct created the strategy that in less than two years generated more than three million new residential and business customers for US Sprint. "We were looking for a way to differentiate Sprint in the mind of the consumer," says Greene. "Long-distance telephone service is sort of ethereal. How do you make something like that tangible? That was our challenge."

Enter the Foncard, an eye-catching, metallic credit card that helped Sprint generate twelve million orders in a year. "With the Foncard, you didn't necessarily have to be a Sprint customer to use it. The card was a way to get people to sample the card as well as let Sprint capture the names of people to be converted to regular subscribers."

The Sprint Foncard campaign was a textbook case of breakthrough direct-response advertising. Devon put the cards in the hands of millions of business travelers by advertising on the ticket jackets of all but two of the nation's major airlines. This technique worked brilliantly because of the "inevitable retention, readability, and reinforcement of the ticket jackets. Travelers must have, hold, and repeatedly refer to the tickets while en route as well as before and after a trip."

EXPANDING THE CUSTOMER BASE

Word of Devon Direct's success with direct-response advertising in the red-hot telecommunications niche spread. The firm is now coordinating direct-response campaigns for Bell Atlantic Corporation, a Baby Bell company; McCaw Cellular Communications, the nation's largest provider of cellular telephones and national paging services; and AT&E, a provider of products and services for technical communications.

Devon has also diversified into such fields as publishing, computer hardware, information services, financial services, and the weight-loss industry. Although their direct-response work for telecommunications companies put their agency on the map, they were far too reliant in the early years on that single industry. "That was probably our biggest marketing mistake—not diversifying sooner than we did," admits Perry.

Another mistake Greene made was "failing to tell my clients who my other clients were. There's the temptation to give clients the impression that they're the only ones you're interested in. But let the clients know. Your client lists establishes your credibility. Other companies like to know that they're with a winner."

When they began to target other industries and companies, Perry says Devon Direct would take aim on the decision makers at the second- or third-leading companies in a category. "The leading company in a field is often more reluctant to try a new marketing approach like direct response. The attitude is, 'If it ain't broke, then don't fix it.' They're more defensive. But the company that would like to be number one figures they've got nothing to lose." The work Devon Direct has done for its clients speaks for itself, and it's through word of mouth that Devon's reputation spreads through the market niches it has targeted.

While word-of-mouth marketing is not terribly scientific, it has worked for Devon Direct, which also uses a New York public relations firm to keep the agency top of mind in the marketing community and the industries where Devon plies its trade. "Once you've succeeded in a niche, people begin coming to you," Perry explains.

No Dog-and-Pony Shows

Unlike conventional advertising agencies, Devon Direct rarely participates in the agency review process—where a client company invites a handful of agencies to present a dog-and-pony show to land its account. "Anyone can respond to an agency review," says Perry.

"You don't have to be very smart to do that. We approach a prospect by explaining that we have a business idea that can increase your sales by a certain percentage within a given time frame. And we can do it cost effectively."

The hard part comes when they explain to a client how intimate they'll need to become with the company's business operations. "It's important for us first of all to know all their marketing objectives and exactly how much they can afford to spend," Perry states. "Ron and I spend a great deal of time with the client the first year. It's an educational process." To facilitate this process, Devon has kept its client list fairly lean to allow the agency's principals to maintain a hand-in-glove relationship with the client company well beyond that first critical year.

Devon Direct does not attempt to compete with general advertising agencies. "Clients need an incredibly good general agency and an incredibly good direct-response agency, but the direct agency cannot be a step-child to the general agency."

While Devon's prime objective is a strong return on investment for its client, image is indeed a by-product of their work. And Devon's work does not lack flair. "Direct response is a rare breed. It's both statistical and creative."

Devon doesn't recruit talent on Madison Avenue. Nearly all of the firm's employees have learned their craft on the client side, rather than in an agency or in the media.

The nonagency character of Devon's creativity is a source of pride for both Perry and Greene, who both say if their firm's success hangs on one secret formula, it's people. "We all came up on the client side," notes Perry. "We speak the client's language. They're more comfortable with us and we're more comfortable with them."

DEVON DIRECT'S TEN SECRETS OF SUCCESSFUL DIRECT MARKETING

1. Who you don't reach via direct mail is more important than who you do reach through direct mail. In other words, have a well-refined list or database.

2. Remember that the people who didn't respond to your direct-mail piece still got an impression of your product or service.

3. Figure the package cost of the direct mail or three-dimensional mailers before briefing the creative team.

4. Spend 50 percent of your time designing the order form.

5. Don't try to second-guess what the customer will respond to.

6. Try to present one succinct idea and force a yes or no response.

7. There is no single element in direct response that is more or less important than the other (e.g., the best creative won't work if the envelope isn't correctly addressed).

8. Ignore response rates—concentrate on cost per order.

9. Use the discipline of direct response as a problem-solving technique for other communications situations.

10. Be wary of any list of ten sure-fire direct-marketing tips. There's no silver bullet to direct marketing success. It takes a lot of hard work.

Telemanagement is sexy. It's about outsourcing and high technology and we think it's a service that's going to keep growing in the 1990s. I've been accused of making it sound too easy, too much fun.

—CAROL KRANE, VICE PRESIDENT OF SALES AND
MARKETING AT CENTEX TELEMANAGEMENT

Centex Telemanagement, which blazed a trail by providing telecommunications management services to small- and mid-size businesses, is beginning to hear footsteps. Carol Krane, the company's vice president of sales and marketing, knows to whom they belong. "They're the wannabes—our competitors," says Krane. "Their problem is they can't seem to figure us out. But the only difference between us and them is that we work harder."

Centex isn't taking the feisty upstarts in the fast-growing field of telecommunications management too lightly, however. The San Francisco-based company is redoubling its efforts to retain clients. To provide more intensive customer service, Centex created the position of CSO, chief service officer, to coordinate the all-important task of customer retention, which has been working. The company's annual retention rate of its clients is 88 percent, a figure that beats industry averages by more than 10 percent.

While the company protects the turf it's staked since its 1985 founding, Krane has been leading her sales and marketing forces on an ambitious expansion into new markets. The company already provides services to companies in six of the nation's ten largest metropolitan areas, including Los Angeles, Chicago, and Detroit. Centex added thirty new sales reps in 1991 to an existing sales force of one hundred, greatly increasing new client growth. Between June and September of 1991 alone, the company signed up an incredible 670 new clients. Most quarters have seen the company add between 200 and 400 companies to its roster of clients.

FINANCIALS WORTH TALKING ABOUT

When Centex Telemanagement sales representatives pitch a new business, they come armed with reports on what stock analysts are saying about Centex. It's not a card every marketer can play, but the analysts like what they're seeing at this company. The analysts' reports are an important element in Centex's marketing mix. "Nobody has financials like us—$24 million in the bank and no debt," says Krane. "Obviously this wouldn't work for everyone." The analysts' reports are not only a source of pride for the company whose sales and net income have been growing by about 30 percent a year but also lend the eight-year-old company third-party credibility. The company, which went public in 1987, is tracked by thirteen leading securities firms, including Merrill Lynch & Company and Smith Barney. Centex's revenues are expected to reach about $190 million in 1992. Outspoken and extremely confident, Krane says telemanagement is "a great business. Our target market is any company with a telephone." The exception is *Fortune* 500 companies because they typically can afford the luxury of handling their telemanagement needs in-house. Small- and mid-size companies, however, find it's far less expensive and more efficient to outsource that vital function. Centex analyzes the telecommunications needs of its clients, selects the best mix of services, and blends the service into a network Centex configures. The company also protects its customers against service breakdowns.

SELLING CONVENIENCE AND PRODUCTIVITY

Centex markets convenience and productivity to the small- and mid-size companies that face a baffling array of decisions over international, long-distance, and local phone service; 800 or 900 lines; calling cards; voice mail; and/or telemarketing services. Krane says Centex customers—known as "members"—qualify for special discounts on a number of special services thanks to Centex's growing clout with the vendors of telecommunications services. "What our members like best is getting just a single bill or the management report. They're wild about not having to sort through all the bills for different services."

Behind the company's impressive growth curve is a lot of hustle and slavish attention to the customer. Krane jokes that the company's marketing success is due to the fact that "so much of the management here is from western Pennsylvania [a coal-mining and steel-refining region], where people are used to working hard for a living." Krane, like Peter Howley, the company's chairman, president, and CEO, emigrated to California from Pennsylvania. They brought the strong work ethic. Each month, Howley hops back in the trenches by taking a turn at the company's Member Assistance Center, where he fields routine service calls. Howley, formerly an engineer for AT&T and then a general manager of a utility company, says the phone work allows him to stay in touch with customers' problems. Because Centex now boasts more than ten thousand customers throughout the country, few get to bend the chairman's ear. In the twenty-five major metropolitan markets Centex has identified for geographic expansion, there are half a million companies with telephone bills ranging from $500 to $5,000 a month. Word-of-mouth referrals drive Centex's spectacular growth. Advertising has not been a major force in the company's progress, not unusual for a company that markets business to business. "We're not a very literature-intensive company. Our sales force is our primary avenue for marketing."

SALES BEFORE MARKETING

At Centex, the marketing function is clearly subordinate to the sales function. That's not to say that the company isn't marketing driven. But rather than rely on reams of market research, focus groups, or long-range new business development plans, the company responds to the instincts of its salespeople, customer service reps, and managers. "We do focus-group research, but our best ideas come from our customers and our people in the field."

To get her ten-person marketing staff to think more like field reps, Krane has the marketers attend a sales meeting at the company's headquarters each month. They participate in role-playing exercises in which they sell the company's services to a "client." If that doesn't get them thinking like sales reps, two weeks in the field does. "Our marketing people need to be exposed to their kind of thinking. The point is to get our marketing people to think more like salespeople. When that happens, the company moves much faster and is more responsive to the market."

A former sales rep who went on to become the West Coast director for MCI Communications, Krane admits that she's partial to the short-term–oriented sales force philosophy versus the long-term, big picture orientation that's more typical of marketing departments. "I drive my marketing people nuts," she says. "But sometimes marketing people want to study things to death. We want our marketing people to move as fast as our salespeople. That's good marketing."

LOW SALARY, HIGH COMMISSIONS

Centex's compensation structure for its sales reps doesn't reward them for ruminating on the big picture. "It's a low base-pay, high-commission structure. Only about 25 to 30 percent of a sales representative's income is salary. The other 70 percent is commission. Their success is measured by member acquisition," or landing new accounts. The reps are drawn from a variety of telecommunications fields. "They may come to us after selling fax machines, voice mail, long-distance phone service, or PBX. We never want them to forget what they used to sell because they remain specialists for us in those particular products. They're very diverse—black, Hispanic, young, old. But they're all self-starters."

Because Centex is selling service, customer service reps and sales reps often visit clients together. The sales rep and the service rep go through the entire order with the member "from the scheduling of the installation to checking all the value-added services such as calling cards or 800 service," says Krane. "They also walk the member through the management report, the critical document because it relieves the member of the burden of managing all the telecommunications vendors and the paperwork they generate." The closing of the sale is also a good time for Centex to sell the member some additional value-added services. And, as a follow-up after the sale is closed, the new customer receives a survey in which he or she is asked to evaluate such things as how well the service has measured up and how well they've been treated by Centex sales and service representatives.

Krane's experience is that the whole sales and service process is best handled by their own staff. "My biggest marketing mistake was when I turned to an outside channel of distribution four or five years ago. They didn't understand our service nearly as well as we did, nor did they share our enthusiasm. My philosophy is to hire your own people and after you do that, get out of their way," says Krane.

A marketer must climb a ladder of success. If you step on a broken rung and trip, that doesn't mean you've failed. You just have to step up two rungs the next time.

—SHELDON ADELSON,
CHAIRMAN AND CEO OF THE INTERFACE GROUP

The man who orchestrates the biggest trade show in America knows what a dicey proposition it can be to launch a trade show in a new market niche. Sheldon Adelson, chairman and CEO of The Interface Group and creator of Computer Distribution Expo (COMDEX)—the computer industry's glittery show of shows, tried unsuccessfully to bring the same brand of razzle-dazzle to the housewares industry and the film business.

In both cases, The Interface Group was forced to fold tent after one exposition. HouseWorld Expo was canceled after its 1987 show in Las Vegas and Cinetex, a Los Angeles film festival and trade show, met the same fate in 1988. Neither of the shows was endorsed by the leading industry associations, a fatal drawback. It's tough to compete against nonprofit trade associations under any circumstances, but when they encourage the industry to stay away, it's almost impossible.

Sheldon Adelson founded the company in 1971 as a small publishing firm. Revenues of the closely held firm now exceed $250 million with about 7 percent growth in 1991. "The recession held us back. I expect we'll resume our normal revenue growth rate of about 15 percent in 1992." The company also operates GWV International, a packaged vacation company; owns Five Star Aircraft, a fleet of L-1011 jets for corporate leasing; and owns and operates the Sands Expo and Convention Center in Las Vegas. Adelson won't discuss profit margins, but will say that the Sands and the company's trade show business are the most profitable elements of the empire.

MARKETING AGAINST THE CLOUT OF ASSOCIATIONS

Industry associations are often well entrenched and have a powerful influence in the trade show business. Depending on the definition, associations are responsible for between 50 and 87 percent of all trade shows. Some associations' sole purpose for existence is to put on an annual trade show. Adelson explains the tensions that arise: "They get paranoid about private exposition producers like us. But we'd prefer not to put on the boxing gloves with trade associations. We'd rather work with them as we do on COMDEX."

The Interface Group, however, is savvy at picking the right niches. "If we see an area that's not being served or if we detect there's discontent with the present show we'll move in." The Interface Group tries to give attendees and exhibitors a raft of value-added services the associations can't hope to match. More important, The Interface Group rounds up the key buyers and sellers in a particular industry and puts them under one roof. "We charge more for our shows, but everyone gets their money's worth. Our package of enhancements includes preregistration of the attendees, booking their trip through our travel group, seminars, demonstrations, news conferences, and a keynote speech by a top person in the industry.

We provide attendees an electronic card that allows them to register at a booth. It cuts down on all the paperwork and helps the exhibitors determine who was at the booth."

PLAYING THE NICHE MARKETS

Although COMDEX is The Interface Group's mainstay product, the Needham, Massachusetts–based company also produces shows in the fields of environmental technology, analytical laboratory equipment, travel and tourism, and emergency management. The company is always on the prowl for new niches, including the transportation industry and the film industry. Given the competition from trade associations, he refuses to discuss specifics in either case, although Adelson, who is not one to mince words, will say how much cooperation he anticipates from the American Film Marketing Association—none.

The Interface Group advertises its shows primarily through direct mail. "We have a fifty-five-person in-house staff that handles our direct mail, trade press advertising, and public relations. We spend many, many millions of dollars on direct mail. We target the top influencers in an industry, many of whom we know from our shows." The key players in the computer industry have to attend COMDEX. The annual fall show in Las Vegas attracts 130,000 attendees, 20,000 of them from overseas. Interface reaches the international market from its offices in Paris, London, Amsterdam, and Tokyo. Nearly two thousand computer companies display their wares at more than eleven thousand booths. Nobody goes to COMDEX to kick tires. Interface's research indicates that 91 percent of the COMDEX attendees make a purchase within twelve months of the show. Many of them are multiunit buyers. The purchase of billions of dollars of computer products can be traced to the previous year's show.

COMDEX has become so big that it no longer plays at a single venue. COMDEX has evolved into several shows within a show. The personal computer industry has divided into vertical markets such as multimedia, *Windows*, and networking—which keeps the show fresh. Exhibitors now set up in the Sands Expo and Convention Center, the Las Vegas Convention Center, Bally's Hotel Casino, the Hilton, the Mirage, and the Riviera. Booking a room? Better do it early, advises

Adelson, a master promoter. "Even with one hundred thousand rooms in Las Vegas, some attendees must stay in Los Angeles, San Diego, and Phoenix and then fly in for the show."

THE GENESIS OF COMDEX

The nation's largest trade show didn't even exist until 1979. That's when Adelson sniffed a marketing opportunity: the emerging computer reseller and dealer channel. Before the introduction of personal computers in the late 1970s, the computer manufacturers were selling only mainframes and minicomputers. Because of their enormous expense and complexity, they were sold by the manufacturer directly to the customer.

"But with the advent of the personal computer and small business computing systems—which could range from $5,000 to $50,000—this new channel of distribution suddenly emerged," says Adelson. To confirm his hunch, Adelson says he "personally went out and surveyed, nose to nose or over the phone, the nation's computer companies. I talked to a couple hundred of the manufacturers to determine what percentage of them were using independent channels of distribution such as dealers and computer resellers. They told me that the number was growing and that my show was a hot idea. At that point, the concept for COMDEX popped up like a jack-in-the-box."

Some of the best market intelligence is gathered by the company's senior managers, who periodically leave their offices to comb the country for new ideas. "We are constantly in touch with everyone. We are extremely demand driven. That's how we find opportunities."

THE INTERFACE GROUP'S SECRETS TO TRADE SHOWS

The Interface Group puts on more than a dozen conferences and exhibitions a year, but none bigger than the spring and fall versions of COMDEX—America's biggest trade show. Here are ten pointers from Interface Group's Vice President Richard Schwab, the behind-the-scenes coordinator of COMDEX and other shows.

1. First you need the germ of a good idea, such as the concept for COMDEX, which for the first time matched the emerging com-

puter reseller and dealer channel with customers and corporate buyers. But more than that, says Schwab, a successful conference and exhibition producer needs to fortify its hunches by talking to industry insiders and editors of the industry trade journals.

2. Create an advisory committee of industry experts who can brainstorm for ideas on making a show different or unusual. In addition to an advisory panel, The Interface Group convenes an editor's panel, which helps identify leading issues and personalities in the industry. The editors may recommend a keynote speaker for the event. Unlike trade associations, The Interface Group is not obligated to adopt all the recommendations of its advisory panels. "The advice from the advisory panel and editor's committee is treated as input that show management will sort out," Schwab explains. "Their advice is invaluable to putting on a successful show."

3. Once prospective attendees and exhibitors have been given a compelling reason to attend, reach them through highly targeted advertising and direct mail. "We carefully select the demographic elements we want at the show," says Schwab. "One of the best ways is to buy the lists of subscribers from the industry trade journals." A team of Interface sales reps assigned to the particular show will follow up with the exhibitors and attendees already contacted via print advertising and direct mail. It's also important to generate preshow publicity by talking to trade journal editors.

4. Book a facility. It's a step that's done well in advance for an established show like COMDEX/Fall which reserves space in major venues such as convention centers and hotels in Las Vegas through the year 2016.

5. Once a regular venue has been established for years to come, do the same with a date or at least a fairly narrow time frame for the exhibition. "Attendees and exhibitors become conditioned to participating in COMDEX/Fall, for example, which always takes place the full week before Thanksgiving. You want them to factor the date of your show into their new product cycles or new product announcements. That helps generate additional publicity for the show."

6. When the groundwork has been laid, show management must concentrate on the logistics, which includes registration, providing security, making identification badges for attendees and exhibitors, and booking hotel and airline reservations for all participants, except for those who choose to do it themselves. "Because we're an integrated show company, we'll handle many more of those elements than associations or private show companies," Schwab points out.

7. Hire a show decorator, a company such as Greyhound Exposition Services or Freeman Brothers, that takes charge of the exhibitors' freight once it reaches the back door of the convention center. In most cases, the show decorator erects the exhibits and sees to such matters as connecting electricity and laying the carpet at the exhibitors' booths.

8. Interface's Conference Department will have recruited the appropriate speakers whose subjects of expertise dovetail with the show's theme. Seminar rooms and speakers' lounges will be designated. Unlike some trade shows that are strictly exhibitions, an Interface show always includes a keynote address by an industry leader and a series of conferences and seminars. "We feel both the exhibitor and attendees will have a better experience," says Schwab, who points out that exhibiting companies can send all their employees working the show to the seminars at no charge.

9. A major show like a COMDEX attracts hundreds of reporters who write or broadcast thousands of stories about new products or marketing strategies announced during the show. "We attempt beforehand to identify the companies planning gangbuster announcements, and slot their news conferences into the larger rooms and often on the first day of the show when interest is most intense," explains Schwab. Interface works with exhibitors to coordinate the times and locations of news conferences, which, for COMDEX, may be more than one hundred. Press rooms are equipped with telephones, PCs, and media kits and press releases from the exhibiting companies.

10. During the show, Interface's market research department conducts interviews to develop a profile of the attendee. Interface not only learns, for example, what degree of purchasing author-

ity the typical attendee has but also collects feedback that allows it to fine-tune the next show to better meet the attendees' and exhibitors' needs. Additional feedback is collected though an attitudinal survey of the exhibitors. Interface interviews those who were invited but didn't attend. As Schwab puts it, "You can learn as much from those who didn't as those who did."

BACK FROM THE DEAD

A FEW YEARS AGO, Rolling Rock beer appeared destined for a slow, painful death. It was a fate many regional brewers faced—as battling brewmasters Anheuser-Busch and Miller brewery wrested an ever-tightening grip on the dwindling consumer suds market. But Rolling Rock has battled back, using a unique "no-bimbos" marketing plan that's helped the Pennsylvania brewer boost sales 15 percent per year.

Sometimes it takes a total overhaul of the marketing policy to turn a dying company around. Shoemaker Allen-Edmonds was, like Rolling Rock, also part of a dying breed. A footwear revolution fueled by Nike, Reebok, and L.A. Gear was putting millions of American feet into soft-soled sports shoes—and dozens of traditional leather shoemakers out of business. But Allen-Edmonds survived by changing its target market and its retail distribution network—and by focusing on producing the world's finest pair of all-leather shoes.

Connecting Point computer stores was in Chapter 11 and millions of dollars in debt, when a new management team moved in to make a final desperate effort to rescue the company. By completely reworking the company's marketing strategy, the new managers turned the retailer around, paid off the debt in full, and sold out for $50 million.

When Myrna Deckert took over as director of the El Paso YWCA, she inherited a staff of eighteen and an annual operations budget of about $100,000. Through meticulous long-range planning and the efforts of hundreds of volunteers from the community, Deckert has helped build the branch to perhaps the nation's top YWCA, with 660 employees and a budget of $12.5 million.

Sharper Image, the catalog and retail operation, enjoyed great success through the 1980s with an eclectic array of merchandise. But somewhere along the line, Sharper Image lost its focus—and its profitability—until founder Richard Thalheimer swooped back in to redirect the company's marketing and merchandise selection strategy.

Faced with increasing competition in the computer terminal manufacturing industry, Link Technologies decided to switch strategies in midstream. The company now specializes in producing customized computer terminals, a timely move that has helped return Link to profitability.

As technology advances and consumer needs shift, the companies that survive and thrive are often those that are most willing to make drastic, innovative changes in their marketing strategies.

Why was the business going down? It was the people. Because the people make the product, the people do the advertising, the people keep the plant clean, and the people service the customer. The biggest problem you have in any business is the people.

—JOHN STOLLENWERK, PRESIDENT OF
ALLEN-EDMONDS SHOES

If you've ever dreamed of stepping into the shoes of the president, you might want to try on a pair of Allen-Edmonds wing tips. Bill Clinton and George Bush have both been known to stroll the Oval Office in their Allen-Edmonds shoes, which, at $200 to $1,600 a pair, are considered by many to be the finest in the world.

The trek from Port Washington, Wisconsin, where Allen-Edmonds shoes are made and soled, to Washington, D.C.—and to thirty-five countries around the world where the shoes are brought and sold—has been no walk in the park for Allen-Edmonds. The footwear industry has stampeded through a revolution the past decade. Nike, Reebok, L.A. Gear, and other high-profile makers of athletic shoes have stormed the market, running literally hundreds of traditional dress shoe manufacturers out of business.

Allen-Edmonds faced that same fate in the late 1970s when an investment group headed by John Stollenwerk stepped in to buy the struggling company from the Allen family. Sales were down and losses were mounting. "It was a typical business-school case of a company losing market share, and continuing to think as a manufacturer—not realizing there were big changes taking place in the world."

SOUL SEARCHING

When Stollenwerk took over the management of the business in 1978, he identified three crucial areas that needed to be overhauled:

- "The first was to turn the operation into a market-driven company. We wanted to get some information about our customers—to find out who they were, and then to tell them about Allen-Edmonds."

- "Second, we wanted to become the finest manufacturer of men's dress shoes in the world. Not just high-quality shoes but absolutely the best—number one in the world."

- "Third, we wanted to become a company of absolute integrity. There was really a lack of integrity in the business—not in the Allen-Edmonds business, but in the whole shoe business. Simple things—different prices for different customers; stores that would damage some of their overstocked shoes just so they could send them back as 'damaged goods'; manufacturers that would delay delivery of orders to one customer so they could fill orders for another more important customer. There was a lot of flimflam going on. At Allen-Edmonds, we just said no more, and we became a company of absolute integrity."

Stollenwerk has faced many challenges since then: in 1978, it was the task of converting reluctant employees to his new management style; in 1984, it was the job of rebuilding the company from the ashes of a fire that destroyed its main manufacturing plant; in 1987, it was overcoming a snub by the Japanese in his attempt to bring Allen-Edmonds shoes to market there.

Throughout the period, Stollenwerk stayed true to his goals, and the results have been dramatic. Even as other shoe companies dropped by the wayside, Allen-Edmonds has racked up record profits year in and year out. Revenues have quadrupled over the past decade. Now with annual sales of about 350,000 pairs of shoes, the company boasts revenues of nearly $50 million.

BREAKING IN THE SHOEMAKERS

Stollenwerk's first step after assuming control of the company was to persuade every member of the four hundred-person work force to buy into his quest for quality, service, and integrity. "That was our biggest obstacle—the people. Why was the business going down? It was the people. Because the people make the product, the people do the advertising, the people keep the plant clean, and the people service the customer. The biggest problem you have in any business is the people."

How did Stollenwerk persuade his work force to stress quality and service? "We got them involved in the business. We made them acutely aware of the customer. We're all customer representatives here. When the phone rings, we pick it up; we find out what the customer wants. The people on the line in our shop also have had to become service-oriented—to make sure that that shoe is correct, that there are no blemishes, that the right shoes are in the right box. Everything we do here is oriented toward servicing the customer."

The service concept was not an easy one for everyone at Allen-Edmonds to accept. Some employees required more convincing than others. A few quit. Others were asked to leave. "But those who remained soon became convinced." Stollenwerk saw his own job as a leader—not a manager. "I don't manage anybody. I manage my phone, I manage my time, and that worker on the line manages his machine, but we don't manage each other. My position is one of leadership."

Stollenwerk proved his mettle as a leader in 1984 when a fire destroyed the company's main manufacturing plant. Virginia Riddle, Allen-Edmonds public relations director, says she and others at the company assumed that meant the end of Allen-Edmonds. "Then John called a meeting of all the workers. He stood up in front and asked all of us to raise our hands. Well, everyone was pretty down and depressed, and only a few hands went up. So he said it again: 'Raise your hands. Everyone raise your hands.' Finally, slowly, everyone put their hands in the air, and John said, 'We've lost our building, but we haven't lost the hands that make Allen-Edmonds shoes.'"

The company quickly rebounded, opening another manufacturing facility nearby. Soon it was back on track, turning out nearly one thousand pairs of shoes a day.

Giving Retailers the Boot

The second step in Stollenwerk's new order was to change the dealer base of Allen-Edmonds shoes. The company stopped selling its shoes in the low-end retail stores and concentrated on high-end department stores like Nordstrom. It also sells its line through high-end men's specialty stores and shoe stores. (It recently introduced a line of women's shoes as well.)

The company has also implemented some incentive programs to encourage salespeople in the stores to push Allen-Edmonds shoes. The top salespeople might win a pair of Allen-Edmonds shoes or a related prize. "In our business, we'd never send somebody to Hawaii or give them a television set," says Stollenwerk. "It has to be related to our business." One recent winner received an all-expense paid trip to Port Washington. The company paid for his lodging, took him out to dinner, and gave him a tour of the Allen-Edmonds manufacturing plant. That may not compare with a Caribbean cruise for two, but everyone enjoys recognition and rewards—and, for those in the shoe business, a personal tour of the plant where the world's finest shoes are made really would hold special significance.

The company has also made a concerted effort to update its styling to appeal to a younger professional clientele. The firm's customer base was growing older and slowly dying. "Every time a hearse drove by," quips Stollenwerk, "we'd say, there goes another Allen-Edmonds customer."

Footsteps Around the World

From the very beginning, global expansion was a key element of Stollenwerk's marketing plan. Foreign sales account for about 10 percent of the company's total revenue.

Allen-Edmonds established dealership agreements throughout Europe and Asia. Surprisingly, Allen-Edmonds shoes sell best in Italy where the competition is keenest. "They appreciate fine-quality shoes."

Not surprisingly, the hardest market to crack was Japan. In 1987, Stollenwerk applied to show his shoes at a Tokyo trade shoe. His request was denied. Although shoe manufacturers throughout Europe were welcome to show their shoes, Americans were barred from the exhibit.

Stollenwerk did not take the snub sitting down. He called a press conference in nearby Milwaukee to lambaste the injustice, packed a trunkful of Allen-Edmonds shoes, and booked a flight for Tokyo.

By the time Stollenwerk arrived, the story was big news both in the United States and Japan, and the embarrassed trade show hosts graciously offered Stollenwerk a booth just inside the exhibit hall entrance. His shoes were a hit, and Stollenwerk laid the groundwork for further distribution in the Japanese market. Japan has since become one of the leading foreign markets for Allen-Edmonds, accounting for more than $250,000 a year in sales.

GETTING THE WORD OUT

Advertising and media relations have been key elements in Allen-Edmonds's success. The company has a full-time press relations director to feed stories to fashion magazines, trade journals, and the general media. It also publishes a glossy eight-page periodical called *Allen-Edmonds Shoe Wrap* that goes to its customers and distributors. Every catalog and every piece of literature the company puts out conveys a sense of uncompromised quality. The company also spends thousands of dollars each month on magazine advertising, targeting the affluent professional market. Allen-Edmonds runs ads in *The Wall Street Journal, Forbes, Fortune, Business Week, Gentleman's Quarterly,* and a number of other fashion and business publications. It also advertises in Harvard and Yale alumni magazines and is heavily represented in the airline magazines. The firm also runs some radio and television spots, although most of the emphasis is on the print media. What Allen-Edmonds emphasizes is the style, quality, comfort, and durability of its shoes. "In the 1980s we talked about how our product helps you get to the top, or how it helps round you off as a perfect dresser or a quality person."

In the 1990s, the emphasis has shifted somewhat, although the stress is still on the quality construction of Allen-Edmonds shoes. One recent ad proclaims: "To Succeed in Business, You've Got to Show the Competition Exactly What You're Made Of." The ad pictures a cut-away shot of an Allen-Edmonds shoe, pointing out the calfskin upper; the leather insole, lining, and heel base; and the other components of the shoe. The copy begins, "Every shoe company claims they make quality shoes. But when asked to support their claims, they offer only flowery prose, or romantic depictions of old-world craftsmanship. At Allen-Edmonds, quality is an easily defensible position. We prefer explaining exactly how our shoes are made. . . . "

Another full-page ad asks, "During The 'Breaking In' Process Of Most Shoes, Exactly What Gets Broken In?" Pictured is a man's well-bandaged foot. The copy begins, "With most shoes 'breaking in' is a painful process. . . ." The ad details the construction and quality of Allen-Edmonds shoes and concludes, "So instead of using the foot as a blunt instrument to pound a shoe into submission, Allen-Edmonds shoes are designed to conform to your foot. Without a fight."

Sticking to Its Stitching

Although the high prices Allen-Edmonds shoes command certainly limit the company's potential customer base, Stollenwerk believes that the high-quality, high-price niche has been the key to the firm's success. "That's what we stand for, that's what we do. And for us, there's probably a heck of a lot better profit margin than if we tried to go head-on against Nike or Reebok. A little company like this would lose its shirt."

Stollenwerk has been adamant about keeping the company focused. "We don't confuse the customer. General Motors has been a classic example of that. They don't know—and the customer doesn't know—what they are to whom. The Oldsmobile looks the same as a Buick, but they try to fool you by putting a little more trim on them or giving them a fancier interior so they can charge you more.

"We would never try to do something like that. Our customers know that when they buy a pair of Allen-Edmonds shoes, they're buying the finest-quality shoes in the world."

Yes, it's important to have a good management team, but it's equally important to have one dynamic leader with a clear sense of purpose—whether it's Bill Gates at Microsoft or Leslie Wexner at The Limited or the late Sam Walton at Wal-Mart—who led the company and gave it its direction.

—RICHARD THALHEIMER, CHAIRMAN, CEO, AND PRESIDENT OF THE SHARPER IMAGE CORPORATION

In just under a decade, Richard Thalheimer succeeded in building the Sharper Image Corporation from a one-man, one-product operation to a nationwide catalog and retail concern with sales of $160 million a year. Then, content in his success and confident in the management team he had assembled, Thalheimer stepped back from Sharper Image to build his dream home and to spend some quality time with his two baby daughters—a decision that nearly cost Thalheimer his company and his fortune.

Earnings at Sharper Image dropped steadily from seventy cents per share in 1987—$12 million in pretax profit—to a loss of twenty-eight cents a share in 1990. The stock plummeted from a high of $10 in 1987 to just $1 in 1991. Thalheimer's personal holdings, formerly worth $60 million, tumbled to just $6 million.

"People told us we should roll over and die," recalls Thalheimer. "I heard every kind of scenario: Change the name of the business, change the concept, close the business, start over."

Thalheimer listened to none of it. Instead he bucked his advisers, overruled his management team, and relied on his own instincts to save the company.

THE AMAZING WALT STACK

A native of Little Rock, Arkansas, Thalheimer worked his way through law school in San Francisco in the 1970s. First he sold *Ency-*

clopaedia Britannica, and later office supplies, both door to door. "Once you've done that, you can sell anything," he laughs.

His first Sharper Image product was a jogger's watch he advertised in *Runner's World* magazine in 1977. The watch sold well, and the returns were encouraging. So, in 1978, he brought a second runner's watch to market, which was to become his first major marketing success. The watch was a chronograph—a wristwatch that doubled as a stop watch—which Thalheimer sold for $69. "This was before digital watches had come out. To get a chronograph that was durable, lightweight, waterproof, and selling at a price that people could afford was really astounding. At the time, there was nothing else like it for under $300."

To market it, Thalheimer ran full-page ads in *Runners World* and several other magazines featuring "The amazing Walt Stack." Stack, then seventy-three years old, is a former seaman—covered from neck to toe with tattoos—and is well known on the marathon circuit throughout the country. "I gave Walt one of these watches to wear everyday during his workout," recalls Thalheimer. Stack's regimen consisted of a ninety-minute run, followed by a thirty-minute swim in the cold, salty San Francisco Bay, followed by a thirty-minute stay in a hot sauna. "This watch would take that punishment everyday, and it just kept running."

Thalheimer's ad read, "The only chronograph that can keep up with the amazing Walt Stack." Sales of the watch soared, netting Thalheimer a $300,000 profit in just one year. (And, by the way, the seaman's rigorous regimen apparently pays off. Like his trusty timepiece, the amazing Walt Stack is still ticking—and still running.)

GROWING THE BUSINESS

Thalheimer used his $300,000 profit to produce a catalog for mass distribution. Rather than rely on just one product, he decided to expand to a broad range of products. To assemble his product line, Thalheimer hit the streets. "I bought some things from street vendors, from art fairs, electronics shows; I might see something in a department store or a specialty store and call the manufacturer. I tried all different types of products, none of which was really related to one another other than the fact that I liked them all. I was the most unsophisticated buyer imaginable. All I knew was how to sell—from my experience selling office supplies and encyclopedias. But I had no idea how to buy anything. I just sort of floundered around."

Thalheimer's "flounderings" ultimately led to an eclectic collection of electronic gadgets and unique collectibles—pulse meters, cordless phones, seashell music boxes, model airplanes, and the like—that gave Sharper Image its early identity.

His first catalog came out in 1979. By 1982, Sharper Image's annual sales had soared to $50 million.

In 1987, with a mail-order client list in the millions, forty-two retail stores across the country, and annual revenues of $160 million, Thalheimer took the company public. His cut was 75 percent of the stock—six million shares at $10 a share. Total value: $60 million.

LOSING THE BUSINESS

It was also in 1987 that Thalheimer began to distance himself from the day-to-day operations of Sharper Image—a decision that nearly cost him his company. "People said that entrepreneurs need to let go, to let their management team take control." That was easy advice for Thalheimer to accept at the time. He was a new father, and he was also hatching plans to build a new dream home. He began to spend more and more time away from the office.

In his absence, the company's earnings per share dropped from seventy cents in 1987 to fifty-eight cents in 1988 to fifty-one cents in 1989. And then, in 1990, the bottom fell out. Sharper Image posted a loss of twenty-eight cents per share. The stock price collapsed, and Thalheimer's $60 million in holdings fell to just $6 million. The precipitous drop caught Thalheimer by surprise. "There was a trend going on there, and it was fairly clear, but I just wasn't reading it." He attributes the decline to several factors:

- "We had allowed our expenses to balloon—to get fat.

- "The unique product collection we had built up through the years was being replenished, not by me, but by other people. And it was losing its edge.

- "As we sold more conventional products, price became more of an issue. People began buying our products elsewhere cheaper. And our margins were lower on the products we did sell.

- "On top of that, the catalog creative was getting very dull."

"So everything was going wrong," adds Thalheimer, "and I, meanwhile, was committing one of the cardinal sins of entrepreneurship by not being as active in the company as I should have been."

WRESTING BACK CONTROL

Thalheimer knew he had to stop the hemorrhaging and stop it fast. His first move was to reclaim control of the company—to step from CEO in hiding to CEO in charge. "Repeatedly, I had been told to step back and let my management team run the company. Yet, as I look back on that advice, I really have to question it. Yes, it's important to have a good management team, but it's equally important to have one dynamic leader with a clear sense of purpose—whether it's Bill Gates at Microsoft or Leslie Wexner at The Limited or the late Sam Walton at Wal-Mart—who led the company and gave it its direction." But reclaiming control of his company was not as easy as Thalheimer had anticipated. The prodigal CEO's return was not met warmly in all corners. His staff resisted many of the strategy changes Thalheimer proposed.

"I finally said, 'Look, I own three-quarters of this company, I'm the one who has seen his stock erode by $54 million, and if, in the end, the whole ship goes down, I want to be at the helm.'"

To bring expenses back under control, Thalheimer cut the staff by 20 percent and eliminated all frivolous perks like the Wednesday morning breakfasts and the free office coffee.

To bolster sales, he brought in a new creative director to spice up the catalogs. And, most important, he resumed his old duties as chief buyer for the company.

SONY NO MORE

Sharper Image had gotten away from the unusual, hard-to-find items that were long considered its trademark. "By 1990 we were buying $22 million worth of goods from Panasonic and Sony—brands that were available everywhere," says Thalheimer. "I decided to eliminate those purchases almost entirely in 1991. But to throw away $20 million in wholesale purchases—about $35 million retail—was considered in our company absolutely heretical, even suicidal. But I was willing to challenge every assertion."

He filled the void with the kind of unique products—cushioned insoles, English walking sticks, miniature weight scales, electronic appointment reminders—that Sharper Image was originally known for. And because the products were unique to Sharper Image, they commanded considerably higher margins than the Sony and Panasonic products.

To ferret out his new blend of offerings, Thalheimer made it a point to seek out the offbeat trade shows—a practice his staff had gotten away from. Thalheimer recalls the irony of the situation. "It was funny, when I'd ask the buyers in my company about a trade show, if they said, 'Oh no, there's nothing there,' that was a clue to me that I should probably go. The shows they thought we should go to were the really big, really luxurious ones with lots of big vendors who wined them and dined them. But that was also where all the other buyers were. We were buying the same things as everyone else. I found that it was at the smaller shows that no one else cared about where I could find the most terrific products."

The other key to Thalheimer's new strategy involved price. With the recession in full force, he decided to pack his catalog with less expensive items, primarily in the $19, $29, $39, and $49 price range.

Customer reaction to the new catalog improved dramatically. The response rate quickly doubled from 1 to 2 percent.

WATERBED IN YOUR SHOE

Thalheimer's biggest seller in 1991 was the Gel Insole, a soft, gel-filled insert for shoes that he discovered at a small trade show in San Francisco. "It was like no other insole on the market. It provided sort of a rolling massage for your feet—like having a waterbed in your shoe." Sharper Image sold the insole for $19. "Nobody in my company thought it would sell. They all laughed at it."

Laughed at it, that is, until the orders started flooding in. By mid-1991, the company was selling the insoles at a rate of thirty thousand pairs per month.

While Sharper Image still posted a loss in 1991, earnings in the final two quarters were up 70 percent from the year before, and the stock price quadrupled from $1 a share in early 1991 to $4 in 1992. Sharper Image was back in focus.

"Detail is what makes retail successful," says Thalheimer. "Now that we've started paying closer attention to detail, and returned to our strength as a marketer of unique products, we've put ourselves in a position to start raising our profits again."

While other brewers have their bimbo posters, we've got these old men with their "33" theories. It really goes against the grain in this business, but it's appropriate for us. It's the way you have to build this type of brand in terms of distinguishing ourselves from the other beers.

—JOHN CHAPPELL, MARKETING DIRECTOR
OF ROLLING ROCK

With consumption down and competition up, the American beer business has become increasingly cutthroat. Industry giants like Anheuser-Busch and Miller beer have been swallowing up a growing share of the market, edging many of the smaller regional brewers out of business.

It was against those odds that Rolling Rock, a popular regional brand brewed in the small western Pennsylvania town of Latrobe, attempted a comeback in the late 1980s. A family-owned operation founded in 1939, Rolling Rock did a steadily increasing business through the mid-1970s, when total sales reached 720,000 barrels a year. It was then that the effects of inadequate marketing began to take their toll.

Rolling Rock sales declined to just 420,000 barrels by 1985 when the Tito family decided to sell the business to Denver-based Sundor Company.

Sundor operated Rolling Rock for a couple of years, raising sales to about five hundred thousand barrels, and then sold the business to LaBatt's in 1987. That's when marketing specialist John Chappell began to work his magic.

BEER WITHOUT THE BIKINIS

Tied to a limited budget in the traditionally high-stakes beer business, Chappell had to come up with some creative ways to distinguish Rolling Rock from the competition. He had no interest in the "Swedish Bikini Team" approach to marketing and no money for the sports celebrity endorsement approach.

In creating a plan, he examined the strengths and shortcomings of past marketing efforts. "This was a brand that had a lot going for it," said Chappell. "The company had always produced a high-quality product. The beer had a very rich, distinct taste. But from a marketing standpoint, the brand was neglected." To refocus the effort, Chappell concentrated on four key areas:

- Price.

- Packaging.

- Promotions.

- Sales force.

"One of the first things I discovered was that our product costs more to produce than other brands, and yet we were selling it for less. That's no way to run a business."

So Rolling Rock raised its price. And sales went up.

The price increase alone, of course, was not entirely responsible for the increased sales, but then again, it did not deter greater sales.

PACKAGING AS ADVERTISING

Packaging played a key role in reshaping Rolling Rock's image. Chappell was allotted a total marketing budget of just $15 million a year—$5 million of which was to be allocated to television, radio, and outdoor advertising. (By comparison, Budweiser spends an estimated $100 million a year in television advertising alone. Miller Genuine Draft spends an estimated $50 to $60 million a year for television.)

To help make up for Rolling Rock's scant ad budget, Chappell decided to get more marketing mileage out of the packaging. "We had to make the packaging an ad for the brand," he explains.

The company gave Rolling Rock's green long-neck bottles a distinctive painted art deco look that stands out in a crowd. "Some people even think the bottles are hand painted," says Chappell. "There's nothing else quite like it. It's different, it's fun; people like to have it on their table." In fact, consumers often insist that Rolling Rock tastes better in the "bar bottles."

The company also redesigned its in-store packages as well. "We wanted to emphasize the long-neck green bottles and the fact that Rolling Rock is brewed from mountain spring water," explained Chappell. "The packaging shows these green bottles in a mountain spring. It's a refreshing, high-quality photographic look." Rolling Rock has some of the best graphics in the beer business. "A consumer can recognize a Rolling Rock package from thirty feet away."

Chappell likes to use the word *charm* in characterizing Rolling Rock's new image. "*Charm*, what does that mean? We think the bottle and the packaging create an endearing feeling. It looks like something that is not mass-produced. It has an innocence about it. And to a great degree, that image matches the beer. Rolling Rock is from this little town in western Pennsylvania. It has one brewery, one water source. That's really different from Anheuser-Busch and even from Coors. Not all of Coors is brewed in Colorado anymore."

How important has the packaging been to Rolling Rock's increased sales? "I'd say it's been critical. *That painted bottle is our key competitive edge.*"

PENETRATING NEW MARKETS

For one thing, the bottle has helped Rolling Rock make a quick jump from a regional brew to a national brand with sales in most major U.S. cities. It has succeeded—with relative ease—where other brands have failed in the overcrowded beer market. "Generally a beer brand has its hardest distribution in the bars and restaurants. Not so with Rolling Rock. That bottle is always popular in the kinds of bars that young professional people patronize. We do very well in cities like New York, Boston, Chicago, San Francisco, and Dallas."

In most new markets, the Rolling Rock sales force will sell the brand to a few key bars. Then it spreads to the off-premise segment (liquor stores). The company does a little advertising, starting with some outdoor advertising and moving to some radio and television spots.

SETTING ITSELF APART

Chappell would be the first to admit that packaging alone won't keep Rolling Rock rolling. "I'd say the packaging accounts for perhaps one-quarter of the influence. About half would be attributed to our other marketing efforts, and the final quarter I would attribute to our national professional sales force."

It's no secret that advertising is crucial to any beer's survival. And in a market that's saturated with sex appeal and macho images, Rolling Rock again has taken a different, distinctive tact.

"Our product doesn't taste like a Miller, a Bud, or a Coors. It's a refreshing beer with a slightly assertive taste. It's brewed today the same way it has been brewed since the company opened in 1939. We've tried to use that in our advertising." Thus the brew's slogan: "Rolling Rock—Same as it ever was."

MEET JOE GARVEY

The company's advertising themes tend to reflect that same low-gloss approach. "Communicating charm is not an easy thing, but we think we've done it pretty well." For instance, many of Rolling Rock's radio spots feature a laid-back spokesman named Joe Garvey.

"Hi," he begins, "This is Joe Garvey, philosopher, beer drinker." Then Garvey launches into a discussion of Rolling Rock and why he likes it. In one ad he concludes, "You may not find the Rolling Rock painted bottle in the Museum of Modern Art, but I think it's just a matter of time." And then overdubbed, "Rolling Rock—Same as it ever was."

THE MYSTERY OF '33

Throughout Rolling Rock's history, the number '33 has appeared on the back of every bottle. No one is quite sure why it's there, but the theories abound. "We get everything from 'thirty-three letters in the ingredients,' to 'thirty-three springs that feed the water supply' to

'Christ died at thirty-three.' We get twenty to thirty letters a week asking about that thirty-three."

What others viewed as a mystery, Chappell saw as a marketing opportunity. "We created this idea that maybe the great geniuses of history would have an answer. What would Freud, Darwin, Beethoven, Galileo, Shakespeare, or Edison think?" The company created posters with the six geniuses contemplating the meaning of '33. Galileo, for instance, saw a constellation with thirty-three stars, Edison saw thirty-three in the filaments of a light bulb.

"While other brewers have their bimbo posters, we've got these old men with their '33' theories. It really goes against the grain in this business, but it's appropriate for us. It's the way you have to build this type of brand in terms of distinguishing ourselves from the other beers."

The campaign has worked well. Despite declining consumption in the beer market, sales of Rolling Rock have doubled since the beer's low point in 1985—from 445,000 barrels a year to nearly 1 million barrels.

"And we expect sales to triple and perhaps quadruple in the next five years," said Chappell. And years from now, if the mystique of Rolling Rock holds true, you can expect annual sales to peak out at about thirty-three million.

One of the things that helped Connecting Point do what it did was an absolute, total, 100 percent, complete, up-front honesty with everybody we dealt with on every occasion.

—GARY HELD, FORMER PRESIDENT
OF CONNECTING POINT COMPUTER STORES

Gary Held has a habit of walking into trouble. He took over as president of Connecting Point computer stores just as the company was entering Chapter 11 bankruptcy. Later he assumed the office of president and CEO of Northgate Computer Systems just as that firm announced an 18 percent drop in earnings.

In both cases, he and his management team managed to pull the companies from the wreckage and return them to profitability—although at Northgate, the cure was only temporary. Ultimately cash flow problems forced the once-high-flying Northgate to sell out to Marjac Investments at four cents a share.

The problem, says Held, is that the computer business is getting more competitive every year. "The technology is changing so fast, and the prices are dropping so fast, that the product much more quickly becomes a commodity product—and when it becomes a commodity product, it's based primarily on price. Ultimately, companies like Northgate will really lose out to the bigger world-class (Japanese and Asian) low-cost manufacturers."

TURNING AROUND CONNECTING POINT

When Held stepped in as president of Connecting Point in 1985, he was part of a whole new management team. The original managers left the company when it filed for Chapter 11.

Upon taking control, the new management team sought—and received—one concession from the shareholders: that the twelve remaining employees and managers would receive 90 percent of the stock if they could turn the company around.

"Connecting Point had never made money, it was $14 million in debt, it had a $10 million negative net worth and it was losing about $300,000 a month. Everybody thought the company was dead, so they agreed to give us the 90 percent."

The next step was to change the entire focus of the operation from store operator to franchiser—not an easy sell in the mid-1980s when computer stores were dropping quickly in the highly competitive market. "We knew we weren't going to be able to sell new franchises, but there were thousands of computer stores already out there that were dying. So rather than to try to open up new computer stores, we needed to convert already-existing computer stores to franchises."

OVERCOMING OBSTACLES

What Held faced was a customer base of independent business owners who already had their own stores, their own store names, their own format, and, in many cases, very little available capital or interest in buying into a whole new program.

"We knew we had to put together a unique franchise program. A normal franchise consists of an entire business format—a name, a look, a product line, a method of doing business, a standard way of dealing with employees and dealing with the public. It combines everything from store design to purchase order forms to accounting systems. It really puts someone in business and gives them all the support and service they need." For that, the parent company exacts a big tribute. ComputerLand, for example, was collecting 8 percent of gross sales from its franchise owners.

With profit margins shrinking and many stores nearing insolvency, collecting 8 percent of the gross sales seemed out of the question. "So we looked at all of the services provided by a franchiser, and broke them into separate services, and decided that we would charge individually for these to an already existing business owner." Connecting Point did not require store owners to purchase any of these services. It was really a matter of forming an alliance with all of the stores without any obligation on the part of the store. Connecting Point offered a variety of services.

STORE NAME

Associate stores could use the Connecting Point name, or they could go by their existing name, adding the subtitle, "A Connecting Point Store." The concept was much like True Value Hardware Stores.

DISCOUNTS ON COMPUTERWARE

"In 1985," says Held, "IBM sold its products to retailers at a 33 percent discount. But if you bought five thousand units of IBM products a year, you got a 40 percent discount." Connecting Point was able to buy the computers from IBM by the thousands at a 40 percent savings and sell them to franchisers at a 35 to 38 percent discount. This gave Connecting Point a profit on the resale, while still delivering IBM computers to franchisees at a better discount than they could get directly from IBM.

ADVERTISING

Connecting Point put together advertising and promotional materials that they made available to franchisees at a much lower cost than they could produce themselves. "If they wanted to use an ad, we might charge them $150 for an ad that cost $2,000 to produce. But if we did a good job on those ads, we might get thirty stores to buy them. That would make us $4,500 in gross revenue on that ad."

SALES TRAINING, STORE DESIGN, AND OTHER SERVICES

Connecting Point offered a variety of consulting and training services—all of which were optional. "Only if we provided a financial benefit or a benefit to the store would they purchase it. Only if our training was good would they sign up for the next round of training." The arrangement kept the burden of performance on Connecting Point and made life a little easier for the store owners.

APPEASING THE CREDITORS

Attracting franchisees was only half the battle for Connecting Point. A more pressing problem was appeasing the creditors. After all, this was a company in bankruptcy with $14 million in debt.

One of Connecting Point's creditors was ITT Financial. "We owed ITT $3 million," says Held. "In order to get the deals with the suppliers such as Apple or IBM, we needed to find a way to pay them. We went back to ITT and convinced them to give us another $3 million credit line. They agreed provided it was in a bonded warehouse where the product wouldn't leave until it was paid for." To shore up the arrangement, Connecting Point had to take several more important steps.

SECURING A WAREHOUSE

Connecting Point approached Bekins International, the trucking firm, and offered them all of their computer shipping business if Bekins would also handle the warehouse business. "They agreed, and agreed to bond in favor of ITT as required, but they required us to find someone to guarantee the warehouse bill."

BACK TO ITT

Connecting Point went back to ITT and convinced them to guarantee the warehousing bill. ITT and Bekins had cross-guaranteed each other—with Connecting Point in the middle.

Over the first two years, the company grew to about 120 stores, enabling Connecting Point to pay off all of its creditors—one hundred cents on the dollar—and come out of Chapter 11. The growth continued to about 250 stores before the management team sold out to Intelligent Electronics in 1989 for $54.6 million, making millionaires of all twelve original employees. With more than sixteen hundred stores, Intelligent Electronics is the nation's largest computer retail chain.

"One of the things that helped Connecting Point do what it did," says Held, "was an absolute, total, 100 percent, complete, up-front honesty with everybody we dealt with on every occasion—even if it meant sitting down with someone and telling them, 'I could tell you I'm going to send you a check for $100,000 every month, but I'm not going to be able to afford that, and I'm only going to send you what I can afford.'"

CASH CRUNCH AT NORTHGATE

Through the late 1980s, Northgate was among the nation's fastest-growing companies—along with a handful of its competitors in the mail-order PC computer business. But cash flow problems and the rapid turnover in computer technology pushed Northgate into financial hot water. The company reported a loss of several million dollars in the second half of 1990. And while it returned to profitability in 1991—under some belt tightening implemented by Held—lack of capital returned the firm to financial trouble in 1992. Northgate sold out to Marjac Investments in the summer of 1992.

Northgate's problems were representative of a technology that may be accelerating faster than the industry can bear. "The product cycle turns too quickly. A product may only be a good product for six to nine months because the technology changes so fast."

The only way to fight it, says Held, "is to modify your offering to differentiate your product and service from the competition. You need to find opportunities that are greater than merely providing the hardware at the lowest cost."

WINDOW OF OPPORTUNITY

It was the rapidly changing technology—and the increasing sophistication of computer buyers—that initially helped make the market for mail-order computer vendors like Northgate, Dell, and Zeos. While no one would have purchased a computer sight unseen several years ago, nowadays a growing share of computer sales are done by phone or mail orders.

"With a new technology, consumers all go to the store to see it firsthand. Initially, nobody bought a CD player by mail order, nobody bought a VCR by mail order. But now they do, because they have become sophisticated enough to know that they want a 'four-head VCR' or a CD player with 'multiple disks.'

"Now that the industry has matured, people buy sight unseen. They call us up on the phone and say 'I want a 486 thirty-three with a two hundred meg ID hard drive, eighteen millisecond access time, and eight megs of memory.' This person doesn't need to go into a store, this person doesn't need to touch and feel and see. This person knows what he wants.

"That's really what created the market for Northgate— the increasing sophistication of the marketplace. As the market-place becomes more sophisticated, the more efficient distribution channels win."

That shift in focus has created severe problems for major manu-facturers like IBM. When a new technology is introduced, IBM must build its new systems, stock its warehouse with the new models, and distribute the new systems to its dealer network—which has its own warehouses to fill and its own existing stock to unload.

"We could get our systems to the market six months before IBM because we custom built every system to order. We didn't keep any finished goods on hand. So when the new technology came out, we put it together, tested it, configured it, and inside of six weeks, we were selling it—months ahead of IBM. That made us look like a tech-nology leader, when in fact, it was IBM technology that we were using in our systems."

Most everyone thinks they plan, but then they don't do the follow-up. . . . If you do your research, develop your plan, involve the right people, and then have someone who consistently stands behind that plan, I think you can accomplish darn near anything.

—Myrna Deckert, executive director
of the El Paso YWCA

When Myrna Deckert was named executive director of the El Paso YWCA in 1970, she inherited a huge new facility and a strong dose of skepticism from much of the community. "If there was any feeling about this new building from the community, it was that it was going to be a white elephant," Deckert recalls. "I heard that around town a lot—'what are y'all going to do with that building?' A lot of people speculated that now that we had built this big monster, we were going to go down the tubes."

But it didn't take long for the community to reassess its initial impression. Under Deckert's results-oriented direction, the YWCA grew quickly, filling the new building and spilling over into several other facilities as well. Now the El Paso YWCA operates six buildings and a twelve-acre urban camp. Membership has grown from about fifteen hundred to fifteen thousand, and the staff has grown from about 15 to 660. The annual operating budget has gone from about $100,000 to $13 million. The El Paso operation is now considered by many to be the top YWCA in America. The turning point for the organization may have come in the early 1970s with the success of a new program it initiated to provide a shelter for homeless girls. The program was so well received it made the cover of *Parade* magazine. "That one article generated a lot of community support. As a result of that, I think people in the community said 'By golly, the YWCA really is doing something.'"

Got to Have a Plan

When Deckert tries to explain the phenomenal growth of the organization, the word she keeps coming back to is *planning*. "Whenever people begin to plan, things begin to happen."

But, of course, the best-laid plans are no guarantee of success. Deckert has been a master at turning a plan into a reality. "Most everyone thinks they plan," says Deckert, "but then they don't do the follow-up. They put it on a shelf. When we put a plan together, we implement it. If you do your research, develop your plan, involve the right people, and then have someone who consistently stands behind that plan, I think you can accomplish darn near anything."

Recently, for example, the YWCA board has been involved in a planning process designed to take the organization into the next century. The process has already consumed more than two years of effort and drawn on the talents of nearly two hundred volunteers. Steps of the process included the following:

- *Evaluation.* The board of directors spent the first year evaluating every program it offered. "We surveyed members, talked to community leaders, interviewed focus groups, looked at all our programs and evaluated the need for each program," says Deckert.

- *Drawing on community leaders.* The board asked several educational leaders and the city planning director to speak on the subject of what they expected the city of El Paso to be like in the year 2010. They were also asked to comment on the role the YWCA should be playing in the community in 2010.

- *Identifying areas of interest.* The board took all the information they collected from surveys and other research and identified eighteen areas of interest that members believed merited additional consideration. Included were such issues as shelters for the homeless, partnerships between the schools and the YWCA, child care, and grass-roots leadership development programs for women.

- *Assigning committees.* The next step was to set up eighteen research committees using about 180 volunteers to determine the role the YWCA should play—if any—in each of those eighteen designated areas of interest.

ACTION-ORIENTED

To ensure follow-up of every plan, Deckert takes a management by objective (MBO) approach. "Every new volunteer and every new staff person is trained in our method of MBO. Every member of the staff has objectives he or she must meet each year. That's the way they get their salary increases—based on whether or not those objectives have been met. When our staff members turn in their monthly reports, they don't report on where they've been or what they've done. They report on their progress toward reaching their objectives."

If there has been one other key to the YWCA's success, says Deckert, it has been the organization's ability to come through with programs that fit a need. "We are constantly asking our members, 'How are we doing? What do we need to do to improve?' If we're going to be in this business, we need to do it right."

By constantly evaluating the needs of the community, Deckert and her board have uncovered a wide range of community voids for the organization to fill. Among other things, the YWCA operates an extensive day-care program that includes eleven centers located in public-housing projects. And it recently purchased a twelve-acre urban camp that will also be used for day-care services as well as for teen recreation programs in the evenings and on weekends.

The organization also offers a variety of other programs geared primarily to women, children, and families. "We use a building block program," explains Deckert. "When we start a new program, we put in a lot of effort, we use a lot of resources, a lot of executive time, and a lot of board time to get it established and fully operational. Once it's established and operational, we move onto something else. That's why we call it a building block program."

=====

Even if you have the right product offering featuring high quality and high performance at an attractive price, you're wasting your time if you can't get it to the right market.

—CHARLES T. COMISO, PRESIDENT OF
LINK TECHNOLOGIES

In the Silicon Valley, where so much of the world's high-tech wizardry is hatched, the manufacturing and marketing of computer terminals is considered rather run of the mill. Known pejoratively as "dumb" terminals—because they rely on the computing power of a separate computer, such as a mainframe—the display devices have been traditionally marketed like a commodity, as if they were lumber or steel or even disk drives.

It was that one-size-fits-all marketing mentality that Charles T. Comiso inherited when he was named president two years ago of Link Technologies in Fremont, California—on the doorstep of the Silicon Valley. Comiso brought twenty years of marketing experience from such high-tech heavyweights as Hewlett-Packard, Texas Instruments, and Wyse Technology to the top spot of the company founded in 1983. He also brought along a very different set of marketing strategies to America's largest manufacturer of computer terminals. "We see our job as a very important one: supplying the interface between the human and the computer. That's what we talk about all the time to our employees and customers. We just don't say we're building and marketing a terminal. I've never agreed with the statement that ours is a mature, commodity product, although the product has many of the characteristics. But we don't feel that way and I think that's why we've been successful here. We have a whole team of people that's rallied behind that feeling."

Link is an independent operating subsidiary of computer hardware marketer Wyse Technology. The San Jose, California–based company manufacturers IBM-compatible microcomputers, PC monitors, and UNIX-based multiuser systems and is the market leader in computer terminals. In 1987, Wyse bought Link, which sells terminals for a variety of applications—from data entry to advanced color and graphics.

But it's more than a rah-rah spirit that helped Link triple its profits and boost its revenues by 26 percent in 1991. Important marketing steps included the following:

- *Customized terminals.* The company began customizing its line of computer terminals for its largest customer segment, original equipment manufacturers (OEMs). (Each of the company's eight new or upgraded lines includes the terminal, screen, and keyboard and mouse.)

- *PR and advertising.* To promote its customizing capabilities, Link uses a multifaceted marketing communications campaign through the computer press, direct mail, and public relations.

- *New distributor network.* Link reorganized and upgraded its distribution channels by signing on several major distributors and six hundred new computer products resellers in the United States.

CATERING TO THE OEMs

Link has grown in the past two years largely on the strength of its marketing to original equipment manufacturers such as Motorola, Unisys, Tandy, and Stratus Computers. In 1991, Link generated $18 million in new contracts with OEMs.

"What Link can do is take a standard terminal and adapt it to the OEMs, and it can do that very cost effectively. Customization is the key to Link's marketing success." For example, Link will make a terminal in any color, add the company's name or logo or throw on any whistle and bell the customer wants. Link has keyboards in fifteen different languages. To send the marketplace a clear signal that Link has escaped the "build it and ship it" mind-set of a commodity marketer, Comiso says the company's sales force emphasizes that its products are designed for easy changeability. "The features and fundamental design of our terminals are such that we can easily adapt it."

Link competes for market share in the terminal market business against the likes of computer behemoths IBM and Digital Equipment Corporation. "There are things we can do for customers by the nature of our size that they can't. A customer may want a small number of customized terminals. We have a sixty-six-thousand-square-foot factory in Fremont that can do that. The bigger players can't do that nearly as easily."

DRIVING HOME THE VALUE-ADDED MESSAGE

To make sure the computing world is getting Link's message that it adds value to computer terminals, the company advertises in magazines read by users of small computing systems. Link's strategy is to create awareness and preference of its terminal products among end users. They will then turn to computer resellers for the Link product to pull the terminals through the reseller channel. The resellers configure the terminals for a customer's multiuser computer environment as well as provide service and support for the customer, typically a company. Sales leads generated by the company's computer press ads are bundled up and referred to the company's distributors or resellers.

Link does not sell directly to the end user. "It's almost a religion with us. Individual end users require a level of support and service Link is neither able nor willing to provide." Link also does not want to create a channel conflict with its resellers, who are a target audience Link can't afford to alienate. About one-third of Link's terminals are sold to computer resellers, also known as value-added resellers (VARs). Link works just as hard to customize a terminal for that customer segment as it does with its OEMs. Link adroitly stresses that point in an ad targeted at computer resellers. The headline reads, "Our business is to make sure they fit yours. Exactly." And the copy, "Most terminal manufacturers expect you to compromise. So they end up trying to convince you that a square peg will fit into a round hole. With standard products that make you sell features rather than solutions. Which is just fine for an off-the-shelf business. But we tend to think that every customer is different."

While Link takes aim on the end user in its computer press ads, its direct mail goes only to lists of the nation's computer resellers, including its own base of resellers. Link also shows the flag on the trade show circuit, although selectively.

Linking a Powerful Reseller Network

Converting Link's new marketing attitude and advertising messages into sales would ultimately fall on the shoulders of its distribution network, which Comiso quickly realized needed some shoring up. "What Link had before were many, many resellers and distributors and resellers. But they were relatively small and didn't have much reach into the marketplace." In the past two years, Link has plugged the gaps in its distribution network by signing on more than six hundred computer resellers. Link also enlisted about a dozen leading computer distributors, who in most cases would supply terminals to the resellers.

Taking the Show Overseas

Link will use much the same distribution strategy to build its international presence. Comiso spent most of his career in international marketing. While with Wyse, he launched that company's international sales and marketing operation. Foreign sales have risen from 7 percent of the company's revenues to 20 percent and Comiso would like that figure to reach 50 percent in another five years. "But we won't do that overnight. We'll gain market share internationally based on the same marketing formula we've used in the U.S. We've picked up some very good business in Europe lately by customizing terminals for four different computer manufacturers. That was something that took us months to nurture, but it's paying off."

Link has also been busy lining up new distributors in countries where it intends to boost its market share. Link now has distributors throughout Western Europe, Latin America, Australia, Malaysia, Indonesia, and Singapore. "Tom Offutt (Link's vice president of international sales) and I both know the international markets very well and we've been able to negotiate some favorable contracts with the OEMs and distributors over there. We will continue to push Link's market presence outside of North America as dramatically and quickly as we can."

Selling Against a Trend

Wherever Link peddles its wares, it must argue its case in the face of a fast-growing trend by companies to network microcomputers or personal computers in a multiuser office setting. Comiso contends that Link's terminals, which have some key advantages over PCs, can be one component of the local area network (LAN) of microcomputers.

"We can put a terminal on the market featuring the cleanest, crispest characters in the industry and a screen that can do color graphics. And we can do that for probably 40 to 50 percent less than what it would cost a business to add a personal computer to that network. We offer the most cost-effective way to get another user on a small, multiuser system." The proliferation of PCs is actually increasing Link's business. For another $400, a business can get another user a seat on the system. It would cost at least $1,000 to add a new computer with enough memory, a graphics card, and a color monitor to do that.

Pricing Strategies

Link is ever-mindful of what it would cost a company to add a PC or a workstation to a LAN rather than a computer terminal. "Our most important pricing consideration is what will it cost a company to use an alternative to a terminal, such as a workstation or a PC, to put another user on their system. We know the price of those alternatives and we have to find a way to be more cost-effective and provide the same result to the end user."

Link has been able to improve its profit margins despite the steady drop in price of PCs and workstations. The two key reasons are:

More features. "We've been enhancing our terminals with more features and performance so the customer is willing to pay the same price or slightly higher."

Streamlined systems. While Link has been making more terminals than ever, it has reduced operating costs with a new streamlined, more adaptable manufacturing system providing more efficiencies, flexibility, and time to market. Product inventories have been cut from $19 to $7 million.

The second frame of reference for Link's pricing decisions is the price of its competitors' products, in particular the terminals made by IBM, Digital, and oddly enough, parent company Wyse Technology. "You also have to keep an eye on what some of the smaller terminal makers are doing."

DELICATELY BITING THE HAND THAT FEEDS THEM

Although Wyse is the market leader in the key segment of general-purpose ASCII text terminal market, with about a 35 percent share versus Link's 13 percent, Comiso doesn't regard Wyse as his company's key competitor. "First of all, they own me," says Comiso with a chuckle. "Wyse has recognized that the computer terminal market is a big one, so why not use a dual brand strategy that allows both companies to reach into the market and grab more share." The relationship is a bit like General Motors, which has several distinct brands of cars. "Think of Wyse as being the Buick line, which does well in the marketplace. But a lot of people also like to buy Pontiacs or Chevrolets or Cadillacs."

But there must be an alternative in any market. "In some cases, the customer base is looking for some product features that I may have, but that the parent product offering does not. Sometimes, we might have a product that Wyse does not because we may be in a different stage of the product life cycle or product development cycle. And I have some features on my product that makes it easier for customization. A customer might come to us and say, 'Hey, we like Wyse, but I need something customized,' and Link can provide that.

"But there are a lot of other competitors out there, which is my point. Even though I'm taking market share, I'm not taking it from the parent organization but from other competitors. And we'll continue to grab market share if we stick to what we do best, which is customizing a product that many competitors treat as just a commodity."

ESTABLISHING
DISTANT BEACHHEADS

INTERNATIONAL BUSINESS IS anything but foreign to U.S. marketers who invest the time to make the contacts and learn the cultures in the overseas markets they've targeted for expansion.

Medtronic, the medical device manufacturer that supplies nearly half the world's heart pacemakers, isn't looking to make a quick buck in its international markets. "We've succeeded in Japan and other countries because we paid our dues," explains William W. George, Medtronic's president and CEO. To be a genuine international marketer, a company must take the battle to a foreign competitor's home turf.

Software marketer Brock Control Systems competes against four hundred companies in the United States with a similar product, but overseas markets are relatively uncharted by the competition. Brock explains which buttons it's pushing in international markets as it grows itself into a $100 million company.

America's leading medical centers are waging one of the fiercest international marketing battles for well-heeled foreign patients. The Methodist Hospital in Houston has established an office of international affairs to spread word of the hospital's long-standing reputation as an international center for leading-edge medicine, which it reinforces with velvet-gloved treatment of the foreign patient.

Sybaritic has learned an important lesson as it tackles the world market: Protect your patent. Without one, international distributors may want nothing to do with your product, reports Steve Daffer, president of the company, which markets a unique health and fitness product called the Alphamassage Energy Sauna.

Knowing the lay of the land is a vital first step to marketing a product or service successfully in international markets.

Our philosophy has always been to compete with our competitors in their backyards. We feel that if we can compete effectively with Siemens in Germany, then surely we can compete with them in the United States or in the rest of the world. But we have to wage the battle on their home turf.

—WILLIAM W. GEORGE,
PRESIDENT AND CEO OF MEDTRONIC, INC.

Although 10 billion yen may sound like a king's ransom, it converts to a more modest $80 million in U.S. currency. But it may be the toughest $80 million Medtronic, a Minneapolis-based medical device company that supplies nearly half of all heart pacemakers worldwide, has ever made.

In Japan, a country that most U.S. marketers find as inscrutable as it is impenetrable, Medtronic is at last flourishing, although it wasn't easy. "We didn't go to Japan eighteen years ago just to rent out an office," says George, who notes Medtronic recently passed the 10 billion yen threshold. "American companies that have gone to Japan will try for a few years, but if things don't go well, they leave. We made a long-term service commitment to build relationships with the Japanese doctors and to their patients." It's an investment that's now beginning to pay off for the savvy international marketer, which collects more than 42 percent of its $1 billion in annual revenues from overseas. Founded in 1949, Medtronic engineers pioneered the first wearable external cardiac pacemaker in 1957 and invented the first reliable implantable heart-pacing system in 1960.

The company also markets heart valves, cardiopulmonary products, and neurological implants that stimulate the spinal cord or the brain through electrical impulses.

A Heartening Milestone

Medtronic has just crossed the 50 percent mark in market share for its pacemaker business in Japan. For the first fifteen years of its existence in Japan it was strictly a marketing and sales company. Three years ago, Medtronic built a manufacturing plant, a research facility, and a major education center on the island of Hokkaido in a little town called Chitose, which is near a major international airport.

"Those investments are a very important part of our overall Japanese strategy. The research center will allow us to tap into Japanese technology, particularly in micro-miniaturization, which allows us to get the smallest possible batteries into our pacemakers. We get access to their talents and that's part of a our global strategy. It gives us credibility with the Japanese doctors because they know we're there to stay. We never leave a country. We sometimes change forms of distribution, but we're very much committed to being there. We've succeeded in Japan and other countries because we paid our dues."

Medtronic's key ingredients to penetrating a foreign market include the following:

- Identifying the leading doctors—their target market—in each new country through international medical conferences and medical meetings.

- Introducing the company to doctors through educational programs rather than advertising and selling.

- Creating a direct-sales and distribution organization in that country, instead of relying on independent distributors to market their products.

Taking It to the Competition

Medtronic firmly believes that to succeed at international marketing, it must take the fight to its competitors' home turf. Four of the world's six largest pacemaking companies are non-American, including two based in Germany, Siemens AG and Bio-Electronic. Medtronic believes that if it can compete effectively with Siemens in Germany, then surely it can compete in the United States and the rest of the world, but it must wage the battle on their home turf.

U.S. marketers that merely export products abroad but never establish a genuine presence on foreign soil are not global marketers in the truest sense of the term, maintains George, who joined Medtronic in 1989 following time as president and chief operating officer of Honeywell Inc. He had been president of Honeywell's European operations during part of his eleven-year career at the company.

"If we're going to be the worldwide leader in all our businesses, then we have to have an equally strong presence outside the United States. It also keeps us aware of what's going on throughout the world. For example, the U.S. automobile manufacturers didn't stay abreast of what the Japanese were doing with their cars because they weren't really competing with the Japanese on their home turf. You have to take the marketing battle there, rather than wait for them to build strength and allow them to invade your home market."

PLAYING THE CHINA CARD

Medtronic's newest international market is China. As in other countries it has established itself, Medtronic's marketing strategy will be to focus on that nation's cardiologists and heart surgeons. "In China, or anywhere, our first approach is clearly one of education. We have hired a number of doctors in China who are coming to work for us as educators. They in turn will travel throughout China to educate doctors about pacemakers and how to implant a pacemaker or a heart valve."

Medtronic will also set up seminars in China's major cities and invite leading heart specialists to attend and learn about their products. "It's really an educational approach as opposed to a selling or an advertising approach. In China, the concept of selling or advertising is not accepted yet, being a Communist country. It would not be appropriate for one of our representatives to introduce themselves as a salesman. That would not go over very well. But if you say your representative is an educator, that would be acceptable. Educators are highly regarded in China. We emphasize that approach in developing countries."

TAKING THE DIRECT ROUTE

It will be years before Medtronic has the physical presence in China that it does in countries like Japan or Germany, where Medtronic operates what it calls Medtronic Germany. Medtronic's German operating company, based in Düsseldorf, "is responsible for all Medtronic products there, from our pacemakers to our neurological products to our heart valves or oxygenators. The German organization has full responsibility for everything in that country, including what used to be known as East Germany."

Medtronic, George explains, does best overseas when it has a direct operation such as it does in Germany, Japan, and the Netherlands. In countries where its presence or market penetration is less evident, Medtronic relies on independent distributors to get their products in the hands of doctors. "However, we prefer to have direct contact with the doctors in our international markets. The doctors know who to call because our reps have built a long-term relationship based on trust and confidence. Also, we get the feedback from the doctors directly back into our organization. If a German doctor, for example, is having any problems, we hear about them instantaneously, rather than having the problem get bottled up or buried."

QUICK TO MARKET

Regardless if the company is marketing at home or abroad, Medtronic moves quickly to introduce a new product. "We believe that technology saves lives. And if we can get that technology fully tested through clinical trials and to our customers ahead of the competition, then we're going to be in a better position to have the leading market share." Medtronic wants doctors to see it as a company that can bring them the most important advances in medicine—to save lives.

Rather than wait for the slow-footed U.S. Food and Drug Administration to approve a new product or therapy, Medtronic conducts its clinical trials in Europe, where the regulatory red tape is less onerous. "We're not taking any shortcuts. Our products or therapies are subjected to a very stringent testing regime that includes animal trials and human clinical trials. Those human trials then come to the United States where leading doctors and teaching institutions determine the safety and effectiveness of the products. But we're going to try to move through them as smoothly and as quickly as we can."

Once the product has passed regulatory muster, Medtronic meticulously trains its sales representatives on the technological aspects of the new product.

WELL-TUNED SALES FORCE

"Our salespeople are well trained technically." The four hundred-member sales force is, in the United States, broken down into thirty-two district offices under the umbrella of five regional offices. The reps are all college graduates; many started medical school and decided they'd rather sell medical devices. All of them have experience with other medical companies.

Supplementing this face-to-face service, Medtronic maintains twenty-four-hour, toll-free assistance programs in which doctors, nurses, and biomedical engineers can get immediate answers from the company's technical experts. The round-the-clock phone service also serves as a hot line between Medtronic's field reps and its technical data sources.

Medtronic bases the price of its new products "in terms of the value of the procedure and consistent with the DRG (the diagnostic related group, Medicare's pricing guidelines for a medical procedure). Prices of existing Medtronic products have remained largely unchanged for the past eight years. "We've absorbed the price of inflation through greater productivity." Despite its flat prices, Medtronic's overall operating margins on a pretax basis are a little bit better than 20 percent.

WORKING FACE TO FACE

Medtronic representatives work closely with their customer-physicians, says George. "One of our representatives is at the doctor's side in the operating room for about 70 percent of the pacemaker implants. That's one of the most important things we do. That might be Sunday night at nine o'clock or five A.M. Thursday. Our people carry beepers and are on call seven days a week like the doctors. It's important for them to be there assisting the doctor with any questions he or she might have about the Medtronic pacemaker."

It's time well spent. "As one of the reps told me, 'When I'm with the doctor in the operating room, my competition's salesperson is not.'" Establishing a relationship with a doctor is not always easy. "Doctors are very busy people. You just don't call them up and say: 'Dr. Jones, I would like to meet you in your office tomorrow at three o'clock.' Odds are they're in surgery or with a patient."

MAKING THE ROUNDS

But Medtronic has learned to adapt to the complicated schedules of its customer-physicians. Its representatives reach doctors in less harried settings such as medical conferences and seminars. The company often sends upward of 150 of its sales reps, engineers, and senior managers to important industry venues such as the American College of Cardiology, the American Heart Association, and the North American Pacing Society. "We can meet with the doctors when they're in a learning mode, and our people learn a great deal by attending the scientific sessions of those meetings." Medtronic also builds relationships with doctors throughout the country by inviting them to the company's Bakken Educational Center in Minneapolis. The center, named for company founder Earl E. Bakken, hosted more than thirteen hundred physicians in 1991. The doctors, who are typically invited by the company's sales representatives, spend several days in training and educational seminars. As it does internationally, Medtronic also sponsors thousands of seminars at leading hospitals and medical teaching institutions around the United States.

Because the company is so focused on nurturing one-to-one relationships with its customer-physicians, Medtronic does relatively little advertising. "What advertising we do is done in medical trade journals, and it's really more of a reminder of who we are. Our competitors advertise more than we do, but we'd rather have face-to-face meetings at medical seminars or in doctors' offices or in the operating room."

A TWO-WAY STREET

The relationship between Medtronic and its customers is a two-way street. "The doctors get the products and service they need and we get some of the best ideas for new technologies, therapies, and new products from the doctors themselves. We work in close collaboration with the more inventive or research-oriented doctors. It only takes two people to design a new medical device—a doctor and an engineer. The ideas then must be translated into fully engineered new products, which doesn't take place overnight. The development cycle is typically two to three years."

About 25 percent of George's time is spent meeting with doctors. "Coming from a nonmedical technology background, I've tried to learn this business from the outside in. And one of the nice things about doctors in our field is that I haven't met one yet who wouldn't give an hour or two to teach me about the things they're working on. It's not that I'm out there with the doctors to make any huge sale. It's more for my education and to learn how we're doing."

CONCERN FOR QUALITY

George is particularly interested in the level of quality the company is delivering along with its products and service. "We operate in a very hostile environment inside the human body. It's an environment that's not well understood. There's a big difference between an industrial product that's designed to work in carefully air-conditioned settings like a computer room versus a heart valve that may be used a billion times inside a human body. That's a challenge and that's why providing quality products and services is the responsibility of all eight thousand employees. That may not be unique, but that sense of customer-focused quality is one the biggest reasons for our success."

You sell a company twice. First of all, you sell them the product, then you sell them the service.

—RICHARD BROCK, FOUNDER, CHAIRMAN, AND CEO
OF BROCK CONTROL

This Atlanta-based software developer figures the best route to becoming a $100 million company lies half a world away. It's in Western Europe, Australia, and the Pacific Rim where demand is intensifying for software packages that can integrate a company's sales and marketing activities.

Richard Brock, founder, chairman, and chief executive of Brock Control Systems, has just the thing for them. It's the Brock Activity Manager Series. "Our product is easily exportable," explains Brock, a hard-charging entrepreneur, who projects that 40 percent of the $20 million privately held company's sales will be overseas by 1995. Foreign sales are currently about 15 percent of the company's annual revenues.

Brock Control, which plunged into the international market in 1988, now sells its product in fifteen countries using seven different languages. There's nothing exotic about Brock Control's attraction to international markets. On the home front, Brock Control must position itself against more than four hundred sales and software automation packages. By contrast, the overseas markets are relatively uncharted by the competition.

FORSAKING THE PEN

"The growth curve is much steeper in Europe, where sales forces are just beginning to automate," explains Wayne Webb, Brock's manager of international development. He joined Brock in early 1991 to help expand the company's international presence. Webb, who speaks seven languages, came to Brock with an impressive portfolio of international sales and marketing experience with such multinationals as Michelin and NEC Corporation.

Many progressive U.S. sales forces have forsaken the traditional pen and notebook for the featherlight notebook computers. Computerized sales forces, armed with the right software, not only have a wealth of information at their fingertips but can provide turn-on-a-dime service to their customers. Companies that have automated the sales and marketing functions have increased sales from 10 to 30 percent.

To penetrate international markets, Brock Control will have to touch all the bases, including locking in the right distributors, showing the company flag at influential trade shows, and getting close to the customer through seminars and users' conferences. Brock says the company will reach its ambitious goal overseas much the same way it does domestically, by striking close relationships with the customer and bending over backward to make sure they stay customers.

MARKETING AN EXPORTABLE PRODUCT

Brock is convinced his company has the right product to succeed overseas. "We can go into the jungle and shine the light on a company's sales process and it's only then that they discover their enormous inefficiencies." With the Brock Control software, for example, field sales, order processing, telemarketing, account management, customer service, and all other business operations enjoy access to a centralized, shared data base. That way, information gleaned from a customer or a prospective customer can be shared with a salesperson in the field or a customer service representative at the home office. Elements of a company's sales and marketing operation have "closed the loop" and no longer act as individual fiefdoms.

VALUABLE CUSTOMER ADVICE

To plumb the needs of its customers, Brock Control created its Users' Advisory Council. The panel, chaired by Brock's Vice President of Services Anthony J. Palermo, includes six customer members who each serve a one-year term. The council, which meets several times a year, is given a big say in how things are done at Brock Control.

Another way that Brock keeps its ear to the ground is through its annual National Users Conference which attracts more than 120 of its 600 client companies to Atlanta each year. The conference gives the customers a chance to speak their mind about Brock's product and service. And Brock Control, which can customize its software to accommodate a client company's individual needs, listens carefully to what the customers want.

CREATING A EUROPEAN USERS' CONFERENCE

Brock Control is exporting that marketing tactic to Europe, where it launched its first-ever European Users Conference in 1991 at a hotel near London's Heathrow International Airport. Attending the conference were several of Brock's international distributors and nearly half of the company's one hundred European customers. Brock Control solicited valuable feedback during the conference through panel discussions and surveys of the customers and distributors.

BUILDING A DISTRIBUTOR NETWORK

The company has been aggressively signing up distributors in foreign markets to sell the Brock Activity Manager. For example, Brock signed a five-year computer software license distribution agreement with Orda-M, a major European information technology distributor based in Belgium. Orda-M now markets, distributes, and supports Brock throughout Europe. In Italy, Brock has concluded a distribution agreement with Temark, a software house specializing in sales and marketing automation. Brock entered the Canadian marketplace through a distribution agreement with the Braegen Group, a Toronto-based value-added reseller. And in Australia, Brock commands 85 percent of the integrated sales and marketing software niche through its high-powered local distributor, Co-Cam Australia. Brock has also struck a distribution arrangement with Banqu' Assur, a Paris-based software house specializing in banking and insurance. "The relationship between Brock and Banqu' Assur expands Brock's position in the French marketplace and encourages the growth of sales and marketing automation on an international level."

Selecting the right international distributor is critical to penetrating a foreign market. Helping Brock Control make the right choice is its network of customers. Brock credits multinational companies such as IBM, Hewlett-Packard, and DuPont, which use the Brock Activity Manager, for helping them identify influential distributors in the countries where Brock hopes to make a splash.

TARGETING THE MULTINATIONALS

It's those multinationals, as well as mid-size U.S. companies that may have recently begun marketing overseas themselves, that Brock will continue to target in its marketing efforts. One lesson that Brock has learned in international marketing is that local companies prefer to buy products or services from local distributors. "A German company is much more comfortable buying from a German, rather than an English or a French distributor."

It's also important to maintain a large presence on the European trade show circuit. Brock and Webb also attend the annual CBIT, the largest computer exposition show in the world. "It's a great place to make industry contacts," says Brock, a globe-trotting pilot who spends fifty days a year on the road talking to customers. In Europe, where trade shows are a more important marketing channel than in the United States, the Brock Activity Manager is displayed and demonstrated at industry expositions by Brock's distributors. Brock Controls' European distributors are also responsible for any advertising or direct-mail campaigns. The more personal the marketing overseas the better, especially for a company that's relatively new on the scene. To target French financial institutions, Brock Control and its French distributor, Banqu' Assur, invited twenty-one prospective customers from that field to an executive breakfast seminar at a seventeenth-century hotel in Paris.

USING SEMINARS

The seminar featured a testimonial by a marketing executive of Hewlett-Packard, which uses the Brock software to market its computer products in France. Brock gave a presentation on how to integrate telemarketing into the sales cycle. Officials from Banqu' Assur described the economic advantages of using a software package to integrate a company's sales and marketing activities. "The net result was two hot prospects," reports Webb. He plans more overseas bread-breaking events to promote the Brock Activity Manager Series.

It's important for a company's executives to rub elbows with customers and prospective customers. In his case, he does it while attending trade shows, speaking at seminars, or selling side by side with the company's U.S. sales representatives or foreign distributors.

While on the road, Brock discovered that the term *sales management* is really an oxymoron. It's the case of the shoemaker's children not having any shoes. "Sales organizations don't do a very good job of selling and marketing." Brock is a former accountant for Price Waterhouse and went on to found a company called Management Control Systems, which sold software to CPA firms. Brock sold the company to a California-based software marketer, but stayed on with the acquiring company as vice president of business development. In that role, he sized up software companies for possible acquisition.

"What I discovered along the way was that most sales organizations did a lousy job of forecasting, organizing territories, getting feedback, following up on sales leads with literature and simply failing to 'close the loop' between sales and customer support and service." The software package that his company went on to develop found a receptive audience in an increasingly cost-conscious world. "Too many companies try to save money by reducing the number of paper clips they use. But that's not the place to save money. It's sales and marketing costs which account for between 15 percent to 35 percent of total corporate costs."

GLEANING CUSTOMER FEEDBACK

Although Brock Controls is only one of dozens of companies selling marketing and sales productivity systems, Brock distinguishes itself in this competitive field through its customer support and service. Each week the company sends "How are we doing?" surveys to randomly selected customers who've called the company's service hot line. The seven-day-a-week toll-free hot line fields about seven hundred calls per month.

The surveys typically ask customers six questions ranging from how quickly their problem was resolved to how well they were treated by the support representatives. Brock reads every survey, lending him further insight into what his customers want.

And therein lies Brock's secret: intense customer attention. "I'm a fanatic about customer service. I don't think enough companies understand the value of hard work. At this point, it's a distinct competitive advantage and one that we claim. It's our secret to success." But Brock concedes that his company's success formula is easy to duplicate. "Our advantage will gradually become less distinct as other companies realize that hard work and intense attention to customer service will be a given in surviving in a global economy."

> *Patent protection is one of the most critical elements in setting up distributorships outside the U.S. When you have it, you feel very powerful. You're as well protected in their market as you are in the U.S. market.*

> —STEVE DAFFER, PRESIDENT OF SYBARITIC, INC.

It is Woody Allen's "Orgasmetron" come to life. Long, sleek, cylindrical, subtly sexual, the Alphamassage 21 warms, soothes, and stimulates the body while it excites the senses with a swirl of scents, sounds, and sensual stimuli. Even at $10,000 to $15,000 per unit, the Alphamassage Energy Sauna is attracting buyers in nearly every corner of the globe.

But in the United States where the machines are produced, only a handful of individuals—including actor Mel Gibson, singer Donnie Osmond, and gum tycoon William Wrigley III—own an Alphamassage.

The slow start in the U.S. market was by design, however, according to Steve Daffer, co-founder and president of Sybaritic, Inc., the Bloomington, Minnesota, manufacturer of the Alphamassage.

"We felt the U.S. was ultimately going to be our largest market, and we didn't want to test it out here first. If we were going to make any mistakes we wanted to make them somewhere else. So we decided not to sell in the U.S., but to sell overseas, and to use those sales to continue to get the bugs out and avoid going into our best market until we were really ready to go."

The Alphamassage is now—at last—ready for takeoff in the United States. The machine was tabbed as best new product of the 1992 Super Show in Atlanta, the largest health and fitness trade show in the world. If all works according to plan, penetrating the U.S. market should be child's play for Alphamassage compared with the tricky task of tackling the world market.

PATENT APPROACH

The Alphamassage is not the first invention of its kind. It's merely the latest hybrid of a long line of similar machines, including the Vibrasaun, an Australian invention that Daffer sold in the United

States for several years before beginning development of the Alphamassage.

The Alphamassage looks remotely like a snowmobile-shaped egg. The top half lifts up like a clam, allowing the user to crawl inside and lie faceup on a soft pad. Then the hollowed top comes back down, covering everything but the user's head. The machine is equipped with dry heat, an ozone lamp, massage vibration, deep back heat, ionized air for the face, and a selection of aromas. It also includes a pair of light-shielded glasses and a pair of stereo headphones that pulsate synchronized light and sound to the user at preset alpha wavelengths.

Although there have been similar machines, there's never been one with all the New Age bells and whistles of the Alphamassage—and Daffer is determined to keep it that way. Long before establishing a worldwide distribution network for the machine, Daffer filed for patent protection—for both mechanics and design—for the Alphamassage in all the major industrial countries.

The company filed for patent protection in two types of countries:

- Countries with high consumer potential like Japan, Germany, France, and most of Europe.

- Countries with knock-off reputations.

"We thought we should get patent protection in countries like Brazil and Korea that are considered knock-off countries," says Daffer. "The only country where I'm not satisfied with our protection is Taiwan. Taiwan is unique in the sense that it is not a member of the world's patent treaty agreement. It is set up to be a knock-off country. Unless you file a patent in Taiwan before you file in any other country in the world, it does not acknowledge the existence of the patent."

Sybaritic has responded by isolating Taiwan's ability to produce for anyone outside of Taiwan. The Alphamassage could still have competition inside of Taiwan, but once knock-offs reach any country that recognizes Sybaritic's patent, the company can block the knock-off's sale.

"Korea has historically been similar to Taiwan, but it has been forced to change due to economic pressure from the U.S. I'm still skeptical. I'm not sure how tight the enforcement is going to be there." Korea is also a very difficult consumer market to crack. "In order for us to export into Korea, our distributor must get an import license for our product, and we must submit to a governmental agency an entire cookbook for our product—materials, technology, parts. They say, 'If you want to sell in our market, you must give us full access to the technology you use in your product.' I'm trying to give them as much as I can without giving everything away."

FINDING DISTRIBUTORS

Getting patent protection is a key first step in setting up an international distribution network. "Once distributors realize that we have patent protection, they know that they have protection from competition in selling that product in their country. In Japan, the first thing they were interested in was whether we had patent protection in their market. When you have it, you feel very powerful.

"A lot of people say patents are poor protection because a good engineering firm can figure out ways to get around a patent. But on the other hand, what that patent does is force that distributor to make a decision early on whether they're going to cooperate with you on a distributorship or a joint venture relationship, or literally relive that entire time and expense that you just went through in developing the product. The patent gives you a definite advantage in the marketplace."

Daffer attracted foreign distributors for the Alphamassage through a couple of channels:

- *Trade shows.* "Trade shows have been the most successful way of finding distributors. We've shown the machine at shows all over the world."

- *Advertising.* The company advertises in two publications, *Showcase USA,* a magazine that goes to distributors all over the world, and *Commercial News,* a magazine published by the U.S. Department of Commerce that also goes to distributors worldwide. "Those ads have helped us find contacts all over the world—Nigeria, Pakistan, Nepal, even Iceland."

DISTRIBUTION AGREEMENTS

Sybaritic has forged distribution agreements in most of the world's leading consumer nations. Typically, the company sets up a one-year contract with distributors that gives the distributor exclusive sales rights in a given area. The contracts, however, include minimum sales quotas. If the distributor fails to meet those quotas, Sybaritic can break the contracts and change distributors.

Finding the perfect match in each country can be a tricky business. While Sybaritic's Japanese distributor has had fair success in moving the machines, Daffer wonders if he might have had more success with a larger distributor. "Our distributor in Japan was very aggressive in pursuing us, but we've been approached since by some very, very big companies like Toyota and Sharp who are interested in being our Japanese distributor. As a result, we may have to change our relationship with our current distributor. On the other hand, we have to be wary of distributors who may be too big. If we tie in with a Toyota or a Mitsui—which do billions of dollars a year in revenue—our machine could get lost in the shuffle."

The firm's best alliance so far has been with a Belgian distributor who has had great success pushing the Alphamassage in Europe. "Our Belgium distributor became so interested in the Alphamassage that he dropped everything else he was doing and made our machine his sole focus in life. He has developed the same intensity and focus there as we have here.

"But you never know for sure what you're going to get when you sign on a new distributor. That's why it's so important to have a well-structured contract that gives us a quick way out of a relationship that just isn't working."

We can help an international doctor through continuing education programs or by making our technology available to them. They know who we are. When it's time to refer a patient to a U.S. hospital, they are more inclined to call us."

—José Nuñez, vice president of international
affairs at The Methodist Hospital, Houston, Texas

Patients from other parts of the world who journey to the leading medical centers in the United States are usually both seriously ill and well-heeled. They're the kind of patients The Methodist Hospital in Houston likes to put in its beds. They're also the kinds of patients health care institutions such as the Mayo Clinic, New York University Medical Center, and the Cleveland Clinic like to treat.

It's José Nuñez's job to see that as many as possible of the cash-paying international patients go to Methodist instead of its prestigious competitors. The senior vice president of the hospital's international affairs office, Nuñez trots the globe marketing the hospital to doctors.

BUILDING ON REPUTATION

Bolstering the hospital's chances of attracting the coveted international patient is its network of fourteen affiliated hospitals from Peru to Turkey, medical symposia in countries throughout the world that feature Methodist specialists and the latest technologies they're using, and the hospital's long-standing reputation as international center of leading-edge medicine and velvet-gloved treatment of the international patient.

"Patients, when they come from another country, are usually admitted for extensive, complicated medical treatment. They're not coming from half a world away for an appendectomy." Because the international patients are typically from the upper economic echelon of their society they can afford to pay for the advanced treatment in cash—a welcome commodity in the age of managed care.

Three percent of the patients at the fifteen hundred-bed hospital are international patients—and the hospital would like more. Patients from more than eighty countries are admitted to Methodist, the nation's largest nonprofit hospital. Two-thirds of the international patients are from Latin America. On the doorstep of Latin America, Methodist is eager to tell doctors and patients in that resurgent region of Methodist's distinguished physicians and facilities.

Nuñez, who comes from a family of physicians in Tegucigalpa, Honduras, notes that sick people from his country have always sought advanced medical treatment in the United States. "Unfortunately, because of the social polarities in Honduras and other Latin

American countries, not many could afford medical attention in the United States."

TARGETING DOCTORS: THE CRITICAL LINK

The critical link between the international patient and the U.S. medical center is the doctor—the primary target of Nuñez's marketing efforts. "The doctors make the decision on where to send the patient. That's why it's my responsibility to establish relationships with physicians. The hospital has always enjoyed a strong international reputation.

"Many foreign doctors have trained at Methodist, so they know us firsthand. We are the primary teaching facility for Baylor University's medical school. Those who don't have heard about us through the news media, which has spread the word about the leading-edge medical care at Methodist. The hospital has enjoyed favorable publicity throughout the world."

Methodist is the home of famed heart surgeon Dr. Michael E. DeBakey and has long been known for its innovations in cardiology and cardiovascular surgery. Over the years, the institution has continued to attract leading physicians and surgeons as well as a roster of distinguished patients that have included sheiks and heads of state.

UNDERSCORING MEDICAL TECHNOLOGY

But Nuñez well knows that the hospital's sterling reputation alone won't get the marketing job done. To reinforce Methodist's image as an international center of medical technology, Nuñez aggressively markets the hospital's technological capabilities and 825-member medical staff—many of whom are leaders in their field. Other key marketing tactics include the following:

- Striking affiliations with hospitals around the world.

- Physicians' visits.

- Traveling medical symposia.

A key international marketing channel is Methodist's fourteen affiliated hospitals around the world. "We have a very strong partnership with the physicians in those hospitals."

What's in it for the physicians at the fourteen Methodist-affiliated hospitals? First of all, the physician's patient gets priority attention when the patient is referred to Methodist for inpatient or outpatient treatment. The doctors are kept up to date on the latest medical developments at Methodist. To sharpen their skills further, an international doctor can spend two weeks at Methodist where he or she is paired with a specialist in that doctor's particular field. "In essence, the Methodist specialist serves as the host to that doctor. It's been a very successful program for both our doctors and the visiting international physicians."

DISPENSING EXPERTISE

Nuñez, who travels extensively throughout Latin America and Europe, arranges medical symposia around the world in which Methodist specialists share their expertise. The symposia, which are built around such specialties as cardiology, neurosurgery, orthopedic surgery, and advanced cancer treatment, have proved to be an excellent marketing tool.

"In developing countries, the doctors are excellent, but they lack the support of a strong medical infrastructure. The doctors in Latin America, for example, are aware of the region's technological limitations." The symposia are not restricted to doctors who practice at a Methodist-affiliated hospital. In countries where Methodist does not have an affiliated medical institution, Nuñez says the hospital will establish relationships with a doctor or doctors. Sometimes, that relationship will lead to a formal affiliation with the hospital at which that doctor practices.

INTENSIVE TLC

Contact with the international patient begins before Methodist rolls out the carpet for them at Houston's Intercontinental Airport, explains Patricia Chalupsky, manager of Methodist's International Patient Services Department. "We'll communicate with them over the phone or the fax to determine when they'll be arriving and also to ask if they have any special needs. You set the tone the moment you begin interacting with the patient." The hospital, whose amenities rival that of a luxury hotel, has an international suite to make the patient feel more at home.

At the airport, international patients are greeted with a sign in their native language. From there the patient is expedited through Immigration and Customs and then escorted to a phone-equipped vehicle where a representative of International Patient Services explains the details of their visit to Methodist.

A twenty-four-hour help line is provided to both the inpatients and the outpatients, who stay at nearby hotels in downtown Houston. "We've had some patients ask us how much they'll be charged for the assistance at the airport and ride to the hospital." The assistance is free. Once they arrive at the hospital, the international patient is assigned a representative who presents them with three miniature flags—one from Texas, one from the United States, and one from their native country. "What the display says to the patient is that the state of Texas and the United States are joining hands to do whatever we can to help you."

CULTURALLY WELL VERSED

The department's three international patient representatives, who speak nine languages, can tap the hospital's community resources network to help with an international patient. The network consists of one hundred of the hospital's employees who have special language or cultural skills. All of the hospital's more than six thousand employees have received some form of training to make them sensitive to the needs of the international patient. The patient leaves the hospital and is returned to the airport with the same degree of hospitality. "We want the international patient to have a pleasant experience so that when they return home they share their experiences with their doctors and friends."

PUTTING THE PRINCIPLES
TO PRACTICE

AMERICA'S BEST MARKETERS personalize and customize, they demonstrate and educate.

They're relationship marketers, telemarketers, green marketers, database marketers, seminar marketers. They're whatever it takes to satisfy their customers.

They're companies like Octel Communications and Brock Control Systems that have formed user groups to advise their executives on what the customer expects from them.

They're service companies like EDS and ADP that know enough about their customer companies that they're entrusted with such sensitive tasks as managing their computer systems or payrolls.

They're companies that have, in the words of Software Publishing Corporation President Fred Gibbons, "aced" all the elements in the marketing mix. "Know them cold," he advises as he clicks them off: "product, price, promotion, distribution, and packaging."

What differentiates the great companies from the others?

ADAPTABILITY

No company develops and launches a new product better than Rubbermaid. Rubbermaid's products are synonymous with virtues like durability and quality, and the company is often first to the retailer's shelves with products that are hits with the consumer a remarkable nine times out of ten. Rubbermaid's secret is cross-disciplinary teams that harness the best and brightest minds in the company. They're given the discretion and latitude to make tough calls in a hurry. It's no wonder they can have a new product to market in as little as twenty weeks.

PRICING

No company has played the pricing game better than Southwest Airlines. The always-profitable, no-frills airline offers air service at one-third to one-fifth the cost of the major carriers. "It boils down to simplicity of operations," explains marketing director David Ridley.

DISTRIBUTION

Can it make or break a company? Link Technology President Charles Comiso sure thinks so. One of the first things he did when he took command of the computer terminals maker was enlist several new influential distributors and six hundred new computer resellers. The upgraded channels contributed to a 26 percent increase in revenues for the company in 1991.

PACKAGING

It's more than just window dressing. Witness Rolling Rock, a beer with a down-at-the-heel, blue collar image that became suddenly fashionable once the brew was shipped in green, longneck bottles with a distinctive painted art deco look that leaves some wondering if the bottles are hand painted. "We think the bottle and packaging create an endearing feeling," explains Rolling Rock's marketing director John Chappell. "It looks like something that is not mass produced. It has an innocence about it." Such charm has helped the once-struggling company to double the number of barrels of beer it sells.

PROMOTION

There have been few as clever as Software Publishing's *Harvard Graphics for Windows* demo disk ad that was enclosed in thirty thousand specially selected issues of *PC Week* magazine. Only those readers who had purchasing authority for *Windows* programs, used business presentation graphics software, and had at least one hundred

PCs at their company received the package. Why waste time and money on prospects that have little affinity for your product? A database can help a marketer separate the wheat from the chaff. Software Publishing's Fred Gibbons didn't include positioning in his list of important cards in the marketing mix. But it would be hard to overlook the positioning efforts of two companies in this book—Nalco Chemical and Pitney Bowes.

CORPORATE IMAGE

Nalco had been in the lucrative but unglamorous business of cleaning the water and purging the pipes of U.S. industry. It was good steady work until the early 1980s, when an economic downturn washed away a number of oil refineries, paper mills, and automotive plants. At about the same time, however, companies became concerned about meeting stricter environmental standards. Nalco, with its years of expertise in treating industrial waste water, discovered a mother lode of new business by marketing itself as a company that could help other companies meet the greener environmental standards of the 1990s.

PRODUCT MODERNIZATION

Pitney Bowes also saw the world passing it by. Its postage machines had acquired a musty, "hand-crank" image. So the company invested half a billion dollars in new product research and relaunched itself as a marketer of high-tech, smart mailing systems that could electronically presort, stamp, and bar code postage to take advantage of U.S. Postal Service discounts. The company is now carrying out the most significant new product cycle in its history.

Every company in this book is also taking a more personalized, targeted approach to its marketing.

TARGET MARKETING

Gerber Products builds a bond with its customers by offering a round-the-clock, toll-free telephone service for people with questions about its products. There are no strings attached. Gerber's not out to capture customer information to plug into a database. The company knows that a distressed parent who can call Gerber at three A.M. to answer questions is probably going to be a loyal Gerber customer for as long as there are little ones at home to feed.

CUSTOMER SERVICE

PC marketer Zeos International handles calls of a different nature on its twenty-four-hour, toll-free technical support line. Although many computer companies offer technical support only during working hours, Zeos scores points with customers by offering advice around the clock. "When people have problems with their computer, it's not always during normal working hours," says Greg Herrick, chairman, president and CEO of Zeos. "We're here twenty-four hours a day—both sales and service."

PROSPECT BUILDING

Devon Direct has capitalized on American business' passion for more targeted forms of marketing. The agency has eschewed the image-gilding practices of traditional advertising in favor of direct response that solicits orders by phone or mail. But there's no silver bullet to direct marketing success, warn agency principals Jim Perry and Ron Greene. Their list of ten secrets of direct marketing ends with this one: "Be wary of any list of ten sure-fire direct-marketing tips."

PRODUCT DEMONSTRATION

With all the high-tech gadgetry on the market these days, seein' is believin'. PictureTel, the world's leading marketer of video conference systems, sponsors a series of half-day seminars throughout the country to demonstrate its wares. As if it were a high-tech séance, a PictureTel rep summons several customers from various points on the globe to talk about the system's advantages. "It's a very powerful marketing program," says sales and vice president Robert F. Mitro.

Even better, perhaps, are PictureTel's private demonstrations known as the "puppy dog approach." "Let them take it home and get used to using it, then see if they can bear to bring it back," explains James Bell, the company's southern region director.

That approach works as well with chicken nuggets as it does with computer motherboards. To persuade a school system to buy its products, Tyson Foods prepares a sample meal of its chicken for schools so youngsters can give it a try. The proof of the pudding is in the eating.

CUSTOMIZATION

Logitech teaches us a lesson about the advantages of customization by taking a prosaic computer peripheral—the mouse—and building one to match a variety of tastes. Logitech makes a mouse for southpaws, a mouse for people with big hands, a cordless mouse, a pilot mouse for first-time users, and a mouse for kids shaped like—you guessed it—a mouse. Could Logitech have sold more than ten million mice had it marketed it as a one-size-fits-all commodity? Probably not. Marketers not only need to better target their messages, but their products as well.

CLIENT EDUCATION

Marketers of medical technology like Medtronic and Biomet prefer to educate their target audience of cardiologists and orthopedic surgeons rather than sell to them. Medtronic and Biomet get their points across at medical seminars, during tours of their research centers or, in the case of Medtronic, at its education center.

GLOBAL MARKETING

U.S. marketers heading overseas would be wise to steal as many pages as possible from Medtronic. The world's leading maker of heart pacemaking devices is looking to do much more than establish a storefront in an international market. Until it's created an infrastructure such as a distribution or research center in a country, Medtronic doesn't believe it can achieve all its objectives. But once it has, Medtronic takes on the competition in its rival's own backyard. "You have to wage the battle on their home turf," George advises. Otherwise, "they build strength and invade your home market."

Although the marketing strategies and tactics used by companies profiled in this book are as diverse as shells on a seashore, they're all attempting to do the same thing: to grow their companies through marketing. It's the way America's best companies will succeed in the 1990s.

INDEX